What the Bible Says about Healthy Living Cookbook

Simple and Tasty Recipes
Featuring God's Ingredients

Hope Egan & Amy Cataldo

Foreword by
Dr. Rex Russell

Heart of Wisdom Publishing

First Edition
Printed in the United States of America

Heart of Wisdom Publishing
200 Coble Road
Shelbyville, TN 37160
www.HeartOfWisdom.com
E-Mail: info@heartofwisdom.com
Fax: 407-246-4563

Visit www.BSACookbook.com

ISBN: 978-0-9819407-0-0

Scripture quotations taken from the *New American Standard Bible*®. Copyright © 1960, 1962, 1963, 1968, 1971, 1972, 1973, 1975, 1977, 1995 by The Lockman Foundation. Used by permission (www.Lockman.org).

Cover & Interior Design: Casey Hooper Design www.caseyhooperdesign.com

ATTENTION CHURCHES, SYNAGOGUES, STUDY GROUPS, TEACHERS AND OTHER ORGANIZATIONS: Quantity discounts are available on bulk purchases of this book for educational, fund-raising or gift purposes, or as premiums for increasing magazine subscriptions or renewals. Special books or book excerpts can also be created to fit specific needs. For more information, please contact the publisher.

Contents

Foreword
Dr. Rex Russell

Good Housekeeping magazine lends its name to certain products by stamping them with the Good Housekeeping Seal of Approval. It's a way to endorse good products for its readers. Similarly, I am pleased to give my "seal of approval" to Hope Egan and Amy Cataldo's *What the Bible Says about Healthy Living Cookbook*. It is, in many ways, the long-awaited companion to my book, *What the Bible Says about Healthy Living*.

First, a little history and a short update on my health. If you read my book, you might recall that I was diagnosed with juvenile diabetes when I was thirteen years old. At that time I was told I could expect to live about twenty more years before serious complications would shorten my life. I immediately had two thoughts. The first was, "Why me?" The next was, "God, use this to help people come to know You." I also clearly remember my mother's response. She said, "Rex, God loves you. You can meet this challenge." She went on to become my constant encourager. Only now do I know how her heart probably ached. Mothers want to fix things, but she could only turn me over to the Lord.

As a boy of thirteen, age thirty-three seemed pretty far off. But each day was a reminder that

I had a serious illness. I had to learn how to give myself daily injections. I had to pay attention to what I ate. I had to be aware of how I felt, and I had to test my blood sugar levels several times a day. I was susceptible to various infections, and I developed numerous cysts and boils. For a very active teenager, diabetes was a very inconvenient illness.

Despite health issues related to diabetes, I lived a fairly normal life. As I look back, one of the gifts that my mother gave me was the mindset to view my diabetes as a challenge. As I grew up, facing challenges was a great motivator. I loved a challenge so much that I was—to put it mildly—competitive in both academics and sports. I played college football for my beloved Oklahoma State University. In my senior year I was named Academic All-American, and I was one of seven students chosen to be a Scholar Athlete of the Year by the Football Hall of Fame.

After I graduated, I attended medical school at Baylor University in Houston. While I was at Baylor I met my wife, Judy, and we were married during my senior year. I did my radiology training at the Mayo Clinic in Rochester, Minnesota, and then I began a radiology practice in Fort

Smith, Arkansas. Judy and I had two sons, and we lived a fairly normal life.

However, at the predicted age of thirty-three, the two big Ds—Diabetes and Death—began their inevitable merger. My kidneys, arteries and eyesight were deteriorating. I continued to have small vessel hemorrhaging in my eyes, and the retina in each eye needed laser therapy every month. The doctors feared that the hemorrhages and laser scarring would eventually lead to blindness. In addition, my legs began swelling, and I developed almost monthly abscesses that had to be drained. The unrelenting and unsightly abscesses became such a source of embarrassment to me that I went to different doctors to have them drained. This embarrassment just added to my overall misery.

Desperate, I searched for anything that might alleviate my health crisis. I exhausted myself searching for medical answers. I gulped down vitamins and mineral supplements—sometimes fifty a day. I searched and researched. With my health rapidly deteriorating, I was depressed, emotionally drained, and spiritually empty. My mother used to tell me, "Rex, when you don't know what to do, just say, 'Lord, help me, help me to figure this out.'" I had used the "help me prayer" so much that it was worn out around the edges.

One evening, I was sprawled out on the couch in a funk—but still with a Bible in my hand. I read Psalm 139:4. The psalmist, in praise, lifted his voice to God and said, "I am fearfully and wonderfully made." I saw no comfort in that claim. I was angry. I said, "God, if I am so wonderfully made, why am I so sick? Why

didn't You give us a way to be healthy?" And then, like a feather making a gentle descent, The Question dropped into my mind: "Have you read my Instruction Book?" No longer the one asking the questions, I felt compelled to answer the one God posed to me. I began a journey to discover what the Bible says about healthy living.

I had a deep belief that the God who created me was also the One who, years ago, heard a little thirteen-year-old boy say, "God, use this to help people come to know you."

The resources for my journey were the Bible, prayer and scientific inquiry. I began to search for hidden treasures, old and new. Since then, I have realized the truth of what a friend of mine often says: "God is a Pointer. He leads by pointing. The first step is ours." God's question, as God's questions often do, pointed me to His Word: "Have you read my Instruction Book?" I started my search somewhat skeptical that there would be any relevant health information in a book that was written so long ago. I was fearful that if I found any answers, other physicians might just roll their eyes in ridicule. But I was committed, so I examined God's Word and any laws and commands that related to health.

The first thing that caught my attention was that God wanted his people to be healthy. He said, "If you . . . keep all His statutes, I will put none of the diseases on you which I have put on the Egyptians; for I, the LORD, am your healer" (Exodus 15:26). This and other verses cemented the idea that there was a relationship between God's ordinances and the health of His people. I began to learn that God had laws and commands relating to health. For example, in Leviticus He instructed the Israelites not to eat pork or shellfish. I wondered if there was some health reason for God telling His people to eat or not eat certain things. I wondered, "Did God have a healing and preventive medicine plan in the Hebrew Scriptures?"

One of my medical school mentors, Dr. Harold Dobson, often said, "When you see something that you perceive as a 'truth,' test it." So I set out to test this pork and shellfish law. Now, let me tell you, I loved pulled pork. I loved pork sausage. I loved ham hocks. I could pile up a plate of shrimp and eat myself silly. I was not too enthusiastic about this test. But I believed I had found truth, and I told God I was going to test it. So I made a commitment to change the way I ate.

My first big test was eliminating pork, shellfish or any scavenger from my diet. About a month into my change, Judy and I realized that my abscesses were gone. I had been plagued by abscesses since I was a teenager. And now I didn't have any? I also realized that my joints did not hurt. Was my arthritis really gone? Intrigued, I continued to study God's health-related laws and ordinances.

About six months into my new eating pattern, I had a setback. Despite my findings and despite my improved health, I was tempted with, of all things, pork sausage. It happened when our family visited my parents in Oklahoma. Something happens in a parent's heart when adult children come home to visit. They want to make their children happy, usually by preparing their favorite foods. Familiar smells coming from the kitchen evoke pleasant memories. For me, it was the smell of sausage wafting up the stairs and sneaking into bed with me. How could I refuse my dad's kind gesture? It would be like turning down his love. He cooked it for me. He cooked a lot of it for me. The simple fact was that I wanted some sausage. So I had a conversation with myself. First, I couldn't hurt my father's feelings. Second, I convinced myself (and told God) that I was just doing another "test" to make sure I was on the right track. By the time I got downstairs, the laughter in the kitchen and the smell of the sausage had mixed and mingled into a swell of childhood memories. I was a goner. I made a pig out of myself eating the sausage, and the next morning my hands were so swollen I could hardly open them. At that moment I was absolutely convinced that there was a health reason behind God's dietary laws. "Thank you, Lord. Thank you," I kept repeating. "Your word is a lamp to my feet and a light to my path" (Psalm 119:105).

But I was a scientist. Would science speak to the adverse health effects of eating pork or shellfish? Would science present any logical reasons for not eating them? As I researched, I found scientific literature that was full of information about the dangers of eating pork and other scavengers. Among other hazards, by their very nature, these creatures are laden with parasites, bacteria, viruses, toxins and infectious agents that can be transmitted to humans. I concluded that God did not intend for them to be our food.

Over my four years of study, God's health

plan slowly began to fit together. Each time I looked at what the Bible said and then found confirmation in science, I would shake my head in amusement and smile with a grateful heart. Truly, we *are* fearfully and wonderfully made. As I studied, I began to organize what I learned around Three Principles. The result was the book *What the Bible Says about Healthy Living*. This book, which has now been published in five languages, focuses on three simple principles that have become helpful decision-making tools for the myriad of readers around the world who follow them:

Principle 1:
Eat only substances God created for food. Avoid what is not designed for food.

Principle 2:
As much as possible, eat foods as they were created—before they are changed or converted into something humans think might be better.

Principle 3:
Avoid food addictions. Don't let any food or drink become your god.

Source: *What the Bible Says about Healthy Living* (Regal Books, 1996).

I faithfully lived out what I learned, and I have since experienced enormous positive health changes from applying the Three Principles to my life. I have not had an abscess in twenty years. I am virtually arthritis free.

Until just recently, I had 20/20 vision. It is now 20/40. Doctors marvel that I don't get infections like other diabetics. I have had the flu only two or three times in the last twenty-five years.

I have also heard from hundreds of people who testify to the health benefits they experience when they simply follow the Three Principles. Many people who struggled with obesity, arthritis, lupus or ulcerative colitis, for example, have shared stories about their health improvements that surprise even me. These and many other illnesses respond to eating the way our Designer intended.

Although I eat faithfully by the Three Principles, I do not presume they are a "cure-all." I still face disease. I still have insulin-dependent diabetes. But the complications of my disease have been reversed and/or delayed. My Creator and Designer, my God and Redeemer is faithful to His Word. He has fulfilled the truth of His Law in my life. He will carry the Truth of His Word to you also.

One might say that at age sixty-seven, I have lived on borrowed time. I would not put it that way. I live each day as a gift—a gift wrapped in the wisdom of God's Instruction Book. We are fearfully and wonderfully made.

About two years ago, I began to suspect a kidney transplant would be part of my future. My kidneys had served me well, but as expected, they were giving out. Finally, in September 2007 I was forced to go on dialysis. It all started when Judy and I were on a cruise with some friends. We planned to go to a book festival in Frankfurt to celebrate *What the Bible Says about Healthy Living*'s recent translation into German. As we floated down the Rhine, we would stop and shop at village markets, gathering what we could of fresh fruits and vegetables. Toward the end of the trip, we stopped at a little village where I purchased and ate a star fruit. That was the last thing I remember. Judy said that the next morning I was confused and that I became less and less alert as the day progressed. We boarded the plane for home, and about two hours into the flight she could barely get me to respond. It became apparent that I was slipping into a coma. The plane was diverted to Newfoundland, and I was transported back to the United States via medical transport and admitted to Massachusetts General Hospital in Boston, where I remained in a coma for six days, lingering on a thin line between life and death. The doctors finally determined that I had gone into a coma from a neurotoxic reaction to the star fruit that I had eaten in Germany.

Star fruit is a yellow five-ribbed fruit that when cut crosswise forms a decorative five-pointed star shape. It has potent antioxidants and is high in potassium, fiber and vitamin A. Star fruit is a healthy snack and poses no problem for people with normal kidney function. However, because it has high levels of oxalic acid, it can cause a deadly neurotoxic reaction in people who have impaired or compromised kidney function.

At any rate, I arrived at the hospital in a coma and was immediately put on dialysis. To complicate my grave condition, I received an injection from a tainted batch of heparin. My body reacted violently as soon as the heparin was injected. The heparin had an immediate and negative effect on my entire system, creating blood clots in various parts of my body and throwing me into intense pain. It damaged my nerves, leaving my left leg paralyzed and my right leg weakened. I remained in the hospital for three weeks and was flown home via medical transport. When I finally arrived home, a long journey of rehabilitation lay before me.

While I was in Boston not knowing whether I would live, a doctor came up to me, patted me on the leg, and said, "You are going to be all right because of the way you've lived." Those words melted into me like refined gold. They became a source of motivation and encouragement in the difficult days that followed. I returned again and again—and still do—to those encouraging words. I never saw that doctor again.

This has been a challenging year. I have gone through extensive rehabilitation on my left leg in order to learn how to walk again. I still receive dialysis three times a week, for four hours each time. I am thankful that I am scheduled for a kidney transplant in January 2009. It will be donated by my son, Randy. I cannot fit words around such an intimate and large gift of love. What can anyone say who is so overwhelmed by love?

My story would be incomplete if I did not mention my wife, Judy. It is our story. I would have literally died without Judy. She has been my rock, my solid and steady friend. She has kept me going when I would have laid down the challenge and just surrendered. She has given me love, companionship and courage on each step of our journey and has made my life shalom, in the largest sense of the word.

ॐ

Shortly after my book was published, many readers asked me to develop an accompanying cookbook. They wanted to apply biblical and scientific concepts to healthy eating, and they needed help to prepare recipes that were based on what the Bible says about food. Because their lives were busy, readers wanted recipes that were as simple as possible. They also wanted recipes that tasted good and were nutritious—"simple, tasty and nutritious" was the battle cry.

I knew a cookbook made perfect sense. But I also knew that a cookbook project was beyond my skill set. My one attempt to make Ezekiel bread did not go well. For some unknown rea-son, it was stone hard and I was tempted just to lick the butter off and be done with it. This experience led me to the realization that a cookbook would have to be the labor of other hands.

God provided.

You can imagine my excitement when Hope and Amy called to tell me they had been inspired by the biblical approach of my book and its Three Principles to develop a cookbook—a cookbook with simple, tasty and nutritious recipes.

I am pleased to say their years of preparing, cooking, tasting and fine-tuning have paid off. I am grateful for their contribution to the *What the Bible Says about Healthy Living* family of resources. It is always humbling to realize that God is creative in the works He starts and leaves nothing lacking or undone. I am enthusiastic in my recommendation of the *What the Bible Says about Healthy Living Cookbook*.

Introduction

"Now what?"

That is the first question most people ask after they read Dr. Rex Russell's popular book, *What the Bible Says about Healthy Living*.

While Dr. Russell's Three Principles provide sound guidance for how to *think* about food choices from a biblical perspective, we are here to help you *take action*.

In creating our recipes, we kept Dr. Russell's Three Principles in mind.

Principle 1: Eat only substances God created for food. Avoid what is not designed for food.

Since our generous and benevolent Father gave us such a large variety of foods to enjoy—all with different tastes, smells, colors and nutrients—we have tried to use a wide variety of God's ingredients throughout this book. And because neither of us eats enough vegetables, our recipes incorporate a lot of them, since they are one of God's most healthy gifts.

Principle 2: As much as possible, eat foods as they were created—before they are changed or converted into something humans think might be better.

We believe that, since God designed our food and He designed our bodies, eating His foods in a form as close as possible to their original state is healthiest. This motivates us to cook from scratch as much as we can, avoid processed foods and ingredients, use whole grains and flours, and buy as many organic ingredients as we can afford.

At the same time, we both "cut corners" in order to be realistic and stay motivated, given life's time constraints. For example, canned beans and tomatoes are staples in our pantries, and this reality is reflected in our recipes. We view eating God's way as a lifestyle marathon to be run and completed, not a short race to be run perfectly.

Principle 3: Don't let any food or drink become your god.

We find that if we follow Principles 1 and 2, Principle 3 often takes care of itself because we tend to feel quite full and satisfied when we eat God's ingredients. While we still indulge in desserts, you will notice that our sweet treats are either fruit based or include honey or maple syrup. These less-processed ingredients are closer to God's original design than refined and bleached white sugar, so they help us avoid swerving down the path of idolatry. Give it some time; your tastes and desires will adjust.

The Bible is filled with examples of people eating together—and even eating with God Himself. Carving out time to prepare home-cooked meals to eat with family or friends often fills the void that eating or drinking to excess tries to fill.

If you are new to cooking—or to healthy cooking—first read "Getting Started" on the pages that follow. Many people get excited about cooking, but they quit if they do not have key ingredients. "Getting Started" includes a list of ingredients to keep on hand for our recipes.

Our first three chapters ("Vegetables, Dressings and Sauces," "Grains and Potatoes," and "Fish, Poultry, Beef and Lamb") are this cookbook's backbone. If you are not sure what to make for dinner, just pick a recipe from each chapter and you will be set. "Meatless Mains" (chapter 4) are not just for vegetarians—they are healthy, economical ways to add variety to meals.

THE RECIPES

We do not think that God expects us to spend hours and hours in the kitchen to prepare the food He gave to us. Besides, few people have time to plan a menu, buy groceries or actually cook as much as they want to. If this sounds like you, do not despair. Our recipes will help you prepare meals that are easy to fix and tastier than what you might expect from "healthy cooking."

Since Amy is a stickler for taste and Hope is (by her own admission) lazy, our recipes had to meet both of our standards. However, just because a recipe is tasty and speedy to us, it might not be for you. For example, chopping onions and garlic might seem tedious to you. Fear not—it will become second nature if you persevere. And, if you are not used to natural foods, the end products may taste different than the foods you are used to (less sweet, for example).

Just remember: Change takes time. Our suggestion? Be patient and feel free to adapt our recipes to suit your needs. By doing so, you will enjoy cooking (and eating) much more.

FORMAT AND FEATURES

Cookbooks that look visually splendid but are hard to follow frustrate us, so with the help of our talented designer (Casey Hooper of Casey Hooper Design), we created our dream format, which is designed to help you easily see what ingredients and steps are involved with each recipe. We also list different ingredient options to give you variety and to allow for personal preferences. When we list several choices (like in *Fruit and Nut Granola,* page 146), a combination of ingredients is often the tastiest. But feel free to just use a single ingredient. Sometimes we give quantity ranges for ingredients—especially for sweeteners and salt—rather than exact amounts. This also allows for personal preferences.

Most recipes include one or more of the following:

- **Divine Design** . . . Inspired by *What the Bible Says about Healthy Living*, these nutritional facts point to God's amazing design behind your food. This information often compels us to prepare and eat healthy foods we might otherwise not try—we hope it will inspire you to do so as well. Regardless of your religious beliefs, you will find these notes interesting. (By the way, you'll notice the little olive branch symbol next to these facts; olives and olive oil represent God's goodness throughout the Bible.)

- **Variations** These changes to the ingredients or directions give you variety and room to experiment.

- **Love Thy Leftovers** These tips give you ideas for unintentional—or intentional—leftovers. For example, if you make a batch of *Basic Cooked Rice* (page 39) for a dinner side dish, the next day the leftovers can be used to make *Fried Rice* (page 99).

While this book includes some nutritional education, please remember that it is just a cookbook. If you are intrigued by the topic of God's design for eating, we urge you to read Dr. Russell's classic, *What the Bible Says about Healthy Living* (Regal Books, 1996).

We pray that this cookbook inspires you to move toward God's design for eating and enhances your cooking and eating experience!

For God's glory,
Hope Egan
Amy Cataldo

Getting Started

We stock our own pantries with the essential ingredients listed here because they help us apply Dr. Russell's Three Principles when we are cooking and eating; as such, they are the staples used in our recipes.

Some of these basics are easy to find; some are more obscure. If your grocery store does not carry an item, request it from the store manager, look for it online, or check for it at a specialty or natural food store.

If you are surprised to find canned or bottled items (such as tuna or salsa) on the list, remember that we use convenience items like these to save time. We believe that keeping us motivated by sacrificing a little on Principle 2 (eating God's foods in their original forms) is more important than trying to eat "perfectly" all the time.

Before adding any item to your pantry, check the label. God's ingredients, rather than man-made or processed ingredients, should be listed first and should be the primary ingredients.

Similarly, certified organic ingredients are generally closer to God's design than nonorganic ones. While it can be cost prohibitive to buy only organic food, we generally splurge for organic meat, dairy products and eggs.

Nonperishable Pantry Items

These ingredients should generally be stored in a cool, dry cupboard, although some (such as grains, beans and flours) can be stored in the refrigerator or freezer.

- **Applesauce.** If you do not have time to make *Applesauce* (page 181), a jar of store-bought applesauce is a good substitute. Look for applesauce that contains 100 percent apples with no sugar added. Use it in *Morning Glory Muffins* (page 145), spread it on *Multigrain Pancakes* (page 154), or mix it with cottage cheese for a snack or light breakfast or lunch.
- **Beans.** We use canned beans (15-ounce cans) for many "Soup, Stew and Chili" recipes and "Meatless Main Dishes." Because beans are tasty, inexpensive and healthy, we always keep several cans in our cupboards: black beans, garbanzo beans (chickpeas), white beans (cannellini or great Northern beans) and red beans (kidney beans). While dried beans are closer to God's design than canned beans, they generally have to be soaked overnight and precooked before using, which makes them less convenient.
- **Broth.** We use boxed broth, since its re-closable top makes it easier to store than

canned. Keep at least one small container (15 ounces) and one large one (32 ounces) in your pantry. You can use chicken, vegetable or even beef, although we use chicken broth for all of our recipes. Beef is generally best used with red-meat-based recipes. Depending on the brand, the salt (sodium) content will vary considerably, which affects how much salt you add, especially in the "Soup, Stew and Chili" chapter. Avoid broths that contain MSG or other additives or preservatives.

• **Canned Tomatoes.** Chopped tomatoes (14- or 28-ounce cans) are used in *Marinara Sauce* (page 32) and many soup and chili recipes; tomato paste is also used in a variety of recipes. If you have the space, other forms (such as tomato sauce) are also good to have on hand.

• **Canned Tuna.** Keep several cans of water-packed tuna on hand for simple, inexpensive lunches and dinners. You can use them to make *Tuna Salad* (page 64), *Mix and Match Pasta* (page 46) or Love Thy Leftover suggestions.

• **Crackers and Chips.** Keep something crunchy on hand to dip into *Black Bean Dip* (page 188), *Roasted Vegetable Dip* (page 189) or *Egg Salad* (page 112). Examples include plain brown rice crackers, corn chips or other whole grain crackers (such as whole wheat or rye). Avoid any crackers or chips containing hydrogenated oils.

• **Dried Fruit.** We generally keep raisins and other dried fruits, such as apricots, cranberries and dates, in our pantries. These, along with figs, dried plums (prunes) and dried apples make great snacks, and they can be used to sweeten breads, cookies and breakfast foods such as *Creamy Brown Rice Cereal* (page 151). Make sure to avoid dried fruit that uses preservatives such as sulfur dioxide.

• **Extra Virgin Olive Oil.** Mentioned frequently in the Bible, olive oil is actually full of "good fats" that aid digestion, lower cholesterol and beautify skin, hair and nails. "Extra virgin" refers to the least-processed way of extracting oil from the olive. If you enjoy Asian food (such as *Fried Rice,* page 99), keep a bottle of sesame oil (or toasted sesame oil) in your refrigerator.

• **Leavening.** Baking soda and nonaluminum baking powder are essential for cakes, cookies or muffins. If you want to bake *Ezekiel Bread* (page 142), you will also need yeast.

• **Lentils and Split Peas.** Filled with protein and flavor, lentils and split peas do not need to be soaked or precooked like dried beans do; therefore, we prefer dried to canned, since they are closer to God's original design. Green or brown lentils (used in *Lentil Loaf with Cashew Sauce,* page 102; *Lentil Salad,* page 104; and *Lentil Rice Soup,* page 122) keep their shape when cooked; red lentils (*Red Lentil Soup,* page 124) become very soft and fall apart easily, as do split peas (*Split Pea Soup,* page 123).

• **Nuts.** Walnuts, pecans and almonds are essential for making *Trail Mix* (page 198), baking desserts like *Oatmeal Raisin Cookies* (page 167) and *Raspberry Thumbprint Cookies* (page 168), and adding to breakfasts like *Hot Oat Cereal* (page 149) and *Muesli* (page 148). Peanuts, cashews and pine nuts also appear in many recipes.

• **Nut and Seed Butters.** Almond, cashew

and peanut butter (salted or unsalted) are quick, flavorful sources of protein and healthy fats. Tahini (used in *Hummus,* page 192, and *Chocolate Peanut Butter Balls,* page 169) is made from sesame seeds. Make sure to buy butters with no added ingredients (other than salt). Natural nut and seed butters have a thin layer of oil on top, which is actually healthier than the hydrogenated oils in processed butters. Once you open the jar, stir the contents and refrigerate the unused portion to keep the oil incorporated and extend its shelf life.

- **Pasta Sauce.** A 24-ounce jar of prepared pasta sauce can be used for last-minute pasta preparation or with recipes like *Spaghetti Squash* (page 20) or *Mix and Match Pasta* (page 46).

- **Rolled Oats.** Also known as "oat flakes" (*not* "quick cooking" or "thick"), rolled oats appear in our "Desserts and Fruit" and "Breakfast" recipes. In some recipes, such as *Fruit and Nut Granola* (page 146), other flakes (quinoa, barley, or rye) are also used.

- **Salsa.** Not only a good snack with corn chips, prepared salsa is also a big time-saver when cooking fish like *Halibut with Salsa* (page 70). It is also a tasty accompaniment to *Sweet Potato and Black Bean Burritos* (page 106).

- **Sea Salt.** If you are used to eating processed foods, you may not be used to adding additional salt when you cook. Because our recipes focus on ingredients that are close to the form in which God provided them, adding salt becomes essential. Sea salt generally has more natural minerals and fewer additives than regular table salt.

- **Seeds.** Sunflower seeds and pumpkin seeds are great as snacks, as a protein-filled salad topper, or as a ground-up ingredient in other recipes. Sesame and flax seeds make a delicious, healthy addition to *Fruit and Nut Granola* (page 146) and other baked goods.

- **Sun-Dried Tomatoes.** These can be found dried or packed in olive oil. If you are using dried, rehydrate them according to the recipe. If you are using oil-packed, just shake off any excess oil, slice them, and add to the recipe. Make sure to avoid tomatoes that contain preservatives such as sulfur dioxide, and make sure any oil-packed tomatoes are packed in olive oil.

- **Sweeteners.** Our recipes rely on liquid sweeteners (honey and 100 percent maple syrup), which can often be substituted for one another. We include a sweetness range for many recipes; experiment to find the sweetness that works best for you.

- **Vinegars.** Wine (red and white), balsamic and cider vinegars are used in many of our recipes.

- **Whole Grains.** Unprocessed brown rice, barley, millet and quinoa are filled with nutrients; we use them in soups, side dishes and meatless main dishes. Millet is yellow, looks like couscous (which is actually a tiny pasta) and can be served much like couscous. Quinoa is the highest-protein grain available. It is not as firm as millet or rice, so expect it to have a soft consistency.

- **Whole Grain Flours.** Whole spelt, whole wheat and oat flours are staples for the baked goods in the "Desserts and Fruit" and "Breakfast" chapters. For greater variety, we also use corn, barley and buckwheat flours in a few recipes. They are not interchangeable with whole wheat or whole spelt, but you can experiment by substituting small portions for wheat or spelt.

• **Whole Grain Pasta.** Although not emphasized in this book, whole grain pasta (such as whole wheat, brown rice or quinoa) is a handy staple for quick meals.

Perishable Pantry Items

• **All-Fruit Spread.** A great addition to plain yogurt or peanut butter and jelly sandwiches, no-added-sugar jam is also used as a sweetener in recipes such as *Raspberry Vinaigrette* (page 24) and *Apricot-Glazed Tuna* (page 69).

• **Butter.** Keep butter (salted or unsalted) on hand for baking, sautéing or spreading on toast. Since it is generally sold by the pound (four sticks), we keep one stick in the refrigerator and the rest in the freezer. If you prefer a butter substitute, make sure to buy one without hydrogenated oils and with the fewest ingredients possible.

• **Cheese.** Feta, goat and Parmesan are the most common cheeses that we use in our recipes. These versatile cheeses can be added to many dishes to enhance the flavor or to convert a side dish into a meatless main dish.

• **Dijon Mustard.** Dijon mustard is used in many main dish and salad dressing recipes.

• **Eggs.** Organic eggs from free-range or cage-free chickens are closer to God's design than regular eggs. Store them in the refrigerator for a quick and delicious breakfast, lunch or dinner, or as an ingredient in many dessert recipes.

• **Garlic.** Garlic is used in many main dishes, soups, sides and salad dressings. Store garlic in a cool, dry place.

• **Ketchup.** You can use ketchup as a substitute for small amounts of tomato paste in many recipes. However, many ketchups have highly processed sugars, so try to buy brands that are sweetened with natural sweeteners rather than sugars or syrups.

• **Lemons and Limes.** Fresh-squeezed lemon and lime juice is delicious over baked fish and in salad dressings. Store lemons and limes in your fruit or vegetable crisper.

• **Mayonnaise.** We suggest using canola- or safflower-based mayonnaise, which is used in recipes such as *Classic Coleslaw* (page 5) and *Classic Potato Salad* (page 54).

• **Milk.** Organic cow's milk or rice milk (or a combination) can be used interchangeably in our recipes. You can also experiment with other milk substitutes, such as almond or oat milk.

• **Onions.** Buy onions (red and yellow) individually or in a 3-pound bag. Like garlic, store onions in a cool, dry place.

• **Plain Yogurt or Kefir.** A common ingredient in dressings and baked goods, organic unsweetened yogurt is a God-given healthy fermented food. Kefir is a drinkable form of yogurt that is used like buttermilk in recipes such as *Multigrain Pancakes* (page 154). Plain yogurt and kefir are generally interchangeable.

• **Prepared Horseradish.** This simple condiment is used in *Salmon with Horseradish Crust* (page 66) and *Tuna Salad* (page 64). Often sold in your grocer's refrigerated section, horseradish with minimal added ingredients is closest to God's design.

• **Soy Sauce or Tamari.** Either product is fine, and the low-salt and wheat-free versions are fine too. These traditional seasonings for Asian cooking are also great in marinades or dressings. Bragg's Liquid Aminos can also be used.

• **Whole Grain Bread.** The most healthful whole grain breads have a dark color. They typically need to be frozen or refrigerated to stay fresh, so the best place to look for healthy bread is in your grocer's freezer or refrigerated section. Or you can bake your own *Ezekiel Bread* (page 142).

Dried Herbs and Spices

If you do not have herbs or spices (or are replacing ancient ones), start with the must-haves listed below. The others are used less often, but they add great flavor in recipes that call for them. For recipes that use the oven or stove, you generally add *fresh* herbs (such as parsley or cilantro) at the *end* of the cooking process; you add *dried* herbs at the *beginning*.

• **Must-haves:** basil, chili powder, cinnamon, cumin, dill, oregano, parsley, peppercorns (and a pepper grinder), rosemary, thyme.

• **Good-to-haves:** cardamom, cayenne, celery seed, cloves, coriander, cumin seeds, curry powder, fennel seeds, ground fennel, marjoram, nutmeg, paprika, sage, ginger.

Equipment

We encourage you to invest in a well-equipped kitchen, since cooking by the Three Principles requires more than a can opener, a microwave and a pot for boiling water. Make sure to stock up on cookware, baking pans, cutting boards, mixing bowls, measuring cups and spoons, wooden spoons and other kitchen essentials. You do not have to spend a fortune, though, since garage sales, thrift stores and even Internet sites (such as ebay.com and craigslist.org) always have acceptable used kitchen equipment for sale.

Here are a few common kitchen supplies that are especially important for healthy cooking:

• **Knives.** Investing in a few high-quality knives will help you enjoy the cooking process. An 8-inch chef's knife and a 4-inch or 6-inch paring knife are essential.

• **Blender and/or Food Processor.** If you can, splurge on a high-quality food processor. Cheaper options are to either buy a "mini prep" and a blender or a combination food mini-processor/blender. Remember, if you want to cut down on the processed food you buy, you will need to process more of it yourself.

• **Rice/Vegetable Steamer.** Once you cook rice with a steamer, you won't go back to stovetop rice cooking. The cooker allows you to set a timer and walk away; it automatically turns itself off. Many rice cookers are combined with a vegetable steamer, which allows you to steam squash for *"Cream" of Squash Soup* (page 128), make *Basic Cooked Chicken* (page 74) or cook other vegetables.

Chapter 1
Vegetables, Dressings and Sauces

SALADS

Classic Coleslaw

Broccoli Peanut Slaw

Tomato Salad

Green Bean and Tomato Salad with
Garlic Basil Dressing

Lemon Herb Bean Salad

Mix and Match Salad

Cucumber Salad

Cauliflower Salad with Sun-Dried
Tomatoes and Olives

Beet Salad

COOKED VEGETABLES

Basic Roasted Vegetables

Maple Walnut Acorn Squash

Roasted Asparagus

Swiss Chard with Pine Nuts and Golden
Raisins

Garlic Ginger Broccoli

Spaghetti Squash

Sweet Potato Fries

Sweet Potato Casserole

DRESSINGS AND SAUCES

Balsamic Vinaigrette

Raspberry Vinaigrette

Lemon Vinaigrette

Caesar Dressing

Creamy Basil Dressing

Cucumber Dill Dressing

Ranch Dressing or Dip

Honey Mustard Dressing

Strawberry Dressing

Marinara Sauce

Pesto

Tomato Basil Vegetable Sauce

SEE ALSO . . .

In the beginning God created . . . vegetables. In fact, in the very first chapter of the Bible He gave Adam all sorts of seed-bearing plants, which included fruits, beans, grains and nuts, as well as vegetables.

> Then God said, "Behold, I have given you every plant yielding seed that is on the surface of all the earth, and every tree which has fruit yielding seed; it shall be food for you." (Genesis 1:29)

Isn't it wonderful that the Creator intentionally designed the exact nutrients your body needs, just six days into creating the world? It's not surprising, since He also created your anatomy and physiology—including your digestive system, which extracts nutrients from this food. In fact, vegetarian food sources are so nutritious that pro-vegetarian arguments are compelling. While we do not agree that God allows us to eat only plant-based foods, we do believe that we would all do well to make these fantastic foods the centerpiece of our diets.

Science confirms that vegetables are one of God's most beneficial gifts to humans. When you avail yourself of this gift, you open yourself to the associated blessings. Vegetables—especially dark green leafy ones and bright, colorful ones—help prevent cancer, reduce the risk of heart disease and heal you from a wide variety of other ailments.

If vegetables are so wonderful, why don't people eat more of them? Unfortunately, many people just don't like vegetables. Although we do enjoy eating them, we usually don't eat enough vegetables because of our busy schedules and because it is hard to keep fresh ones on hand. The best way we have found to boost our vegetable intake is to eat raw or cooked veggies in our sandwiches, omelets, rice dishes, casseroles and anywhere else we can. Throughout this book, you'll find plenty of ideas for doing this. In addition, this chapter provides recipes for side dishes and salad dressings that can help you boost your veggie intake. For example, making *Balsamic Vinaigrette* or *Raspberry Vinaigrette* can actually help you look forward to eating salads. By adding sliced pears, pecans, dried cranberries and some feta cheese, as suggested in *Mix and Match Salad*, you can create an entrée salad that beats any restaurant's!

Principle 1

Thank God for giving you so many vegetables with
so many tastes, smells, textures, colors and benefits.

Principle 2

God gave you vegetables—including the peels—
for your health. Keeping the skins on, choosing organic
produce and eating vegetables raw or only lightly steamed
will help you reap the most of God's intended benefits.

Principle 3

Vegetables are the one food that is hard to
eat too much of. If you find yourself idolizing them,
consider yourself blessed—but repent anyhow.

Classic Coleslaw

Makes about 8 cups.

COLESLAW

½ medium cabbage (green, red or a combination)

3 unpeeled carrots

1 small onion (red or yellow) or 3 to 4 green onions (white and some green)

DRESSING

½ cup plain yogurt

½ cup mayonnaise

1 tablespoon prepared horseradish

2 tablespoons white wine vinegar

1 to 2 tablespoons honey

2 teaspoons Dijon mustard

½ teaspoon celery or caraway seeds

¼ to ½ teaspoon salt

Several generous grindings of pepper

OPTIONAL INGREDIENTS (PICK ONE)

- 1 unpeeled apple, shredded
- 1 small jicama, peeled and shredded
- 1 to 2 broccoli stalks, peeled and shredded

1. Shred the cabbage in a food processor and transfer to a large bowl.

2. Repeat step 1 with the carrots and any optional ingredients.

3. Finely chop the onion and add to the bowl.

4. In a small bowl combine the dressing ingredients and mix well to incorporate.

5. Pour the dressing mixture over the vegetable mixture and mix well to incorporate. If you have the time, chill at least 1 hour before serving.

Variations

- Substitute 7 cups preshredded coleslaw or broccoli slaw mix for the cabbage and carrots.

- For finely diced coleslaw, use the food processor's metal blade to chop the carrots and cabbage instead of shredding them.

- Instead of making your own dressing, toss the shredded cabbage and other vegetables with dressing leftover from *Chicken Salad with Pecans and Grapes* (page 75) or store-bought poppy seed dressing.

- Add ⅓ cup raisins and/or sunflower seeds to the bowl in step 4.

- Experiment with different proportions of yogurt and mayonnaise.

 Love Thy Leftovers

Use leftover coleslaw as a sandwich spread.

Broccoli Peanut Slaw

Makes about 10 cups.

COLESLAW
1 bunch broccoli (about 1½ pounds)

1 or 2 unpeeled carrots

1 small onion

1 cup peanuts

1 cup raisins

DRESSING
⅓ cup extra virgin olive oil

¼ cup honey

¼ cup cider vinegar

1 teaspoon celery seed

¼ to ½ teaspoon salt

1 teaspoon Dijon mustard

Several generous grindings of pepper

1. Cut off the bottom inch of the broccoli stems and discard.

2. Shred the broccoli (florets and stems) in a food processor and transfer to a large bowl. Do the same with the carrots.

3. Finely chop the onion and add to the bowl.

4. Chop the peanuts and add to the bowl, along with the raisins.

5. Combine the dressing ingredients in a small glass jar and shake well, or whisk together in a small bowl.

6. Pour the dressing over the vegetable mixture and mix well to incorporate.

7. If you have the time, chill at least 1 hour before serving.

Divine Design: Broccoli

Every two minutes another woman is diagnosed with breast cancer in the United States. But God is the giver of abundant hope and a future (Jeremiah 29:11). He does not leave you defenseless. Add this custom-designed warrior to your daily veggie intake to use its powerful cancer-fighting attributes.

Variations

- Substitute 8 cups preshredded broccoli slaw or coleslaw mix for the broccoli and carrots, or substitute shredded cabbage for the broccoli.

- Substitute ¾ cup sunflower seeds for the peanuts.

- Finely dice the broccoli instead of shredding it.

- Experiment by adding fresh chopped herbs, such as cilantro or basil.

Love Thy Leftovers

- Add *Basic Cooked Chicken* (page 74) to leftover Broccoli Peanut Slaw.

- Combine ½ cup leftover Broccoli Peanut Slaw and ¼ cup *Basic Cooked Rice* (page 39) to make an easy lunch sandwich or wrap.

Tomato Salad

Makes about 4 cups.

4 ripe tomatoes (or 2 pints grape or cherry tomatoes)

1 garlic clove
⅛ to ¼ medium onion

15 fresh basil leaves
15 fresh mint leaves

2 tablespoons extra virgin olive oil
1 tablespoon balsamic vinegar
2 tablespoons feta cheese (1 to 2 ounces)
Several dashes of salt
Several generous grindings of pepper

1. Cut the tomatoes into bite-sized pieces and place into a medium bowl. (If you are using grape tomatoes, cut them into quarters or halves.)

2. Finely chop the garlic and onion and add to the bowl.

3. Finely chop the basil and mint leaves and add to the bowl.

4. Add the remaining ingredients to the bowl. Gently mix together. Serve chilled or at room temperature.

Divine Design: Tomatoes

When shopping for tomatoes, don't go for green. The ripe red fruits have four times the beta-carotene of their pale counterparts. Even canned tomatoes contain the full amount of this God-given antioxidant.

Variation

For a Middle Eastern version of this salad, omit the feta cheese, substitute parsley for the basil, substitute lemon juice for the balsamic vinegar, and add a chopped ¼ cucumber. Adjust seasonings to taste.

Green Bean and Tomato Salad with Garlic Basil Dressing

This recipe makes more dressing than you need for the salad; see Love Thy Leftovers for ways to use it.

Makes about 8 servings.

2 pounds green beans

1 garlic clove
⅛ medium red onion
2 tablespoons Dijon mustard
2 tablespoons red wine vinegar
¼ to ½ teaspoon salt
Several generous grindings of pepper
15 fresh basil leaves
¾ cup extra virgin olive oil

1 pint grape or cherry tomatoes

1. Break off the stem ends from the green beans.

2. Steam the beans until they are barely tender, about 8 to 10 minutes.

3. While the beans are cooking, prepare the dressing:

   a. Finely chop the garlic and onion in a food processor or blender.

   b. Add the mustard, vinegar, salt, pepper and basil, and process until well combined.

   c. While the processor is running, slowly pour the olive oil through the feed tube and blend until smooth.

4. As soon as the beans are done, rinse with cold water and drain well.

5. Transfer the beans to a large bowl. Add the tomatoes and about half the dressing. Toss gently until the beans are well coated.

6. If desired, drizzle with extra dressing before serving.

Divine Design: Green Beans

The Creator gave you many nutrients to keep your body thriving. God filled green beans with cancer-fighting antioxidants vitamin A and vitamin C. For a healthy heart, He provided potassium, manganese and fiber.

 ## Variation

Serve the green beans and tomatoes over a bed of greens.

 ## Love Thy Leftovers

- Add a can of tuna (drained and flaked), thinly sliced red onions and leftover potatoes, and toss with any leftover dressing.

- The remaining dressing can be used as a marinade for chicken, a dressing for other salads or a sauce for steamed veggies or fish.

Lemon Herb Bean Salad

Makes 7 to 8 cups.

SALAD

½ pint grape or cherry tomatoes

½ red bell pepper

½ red onion

¼ bunch parsley (mostly leaves)

1, 15-ounce can of kidney beans, rinsed and drained

1, 15-ounce can of garbanzo beans, rinsed and drained

1, 14-once can of artichoke hearts packed in water, drained and quartered

LEMON HERB DRESSING

1 garlic clove

Juice of ½ lemon (about 2 tablespoons)

1 tablespoon extra virgin olive oil

1 tablespoon balsamic vinegar

1½ teaspoons Dijon mustard

1 teaspoon dried basil

1 teaspoon dried oregano

½ teaspoon dried thyme

¼ teaspoon salt

Several generous grindings of pepper

1. Halve or quarter the tomatoes, dice the pepper and onion, and chop the parsley. Add to a large bowl.

2. Rinse and drain the beans and artichokes, and add to the bowl.

3. Combine the dressing ingredients in a small glass jar and shake well, or whisk together in a small bowl.

4. Pour the dressing over the salad and mix to incorporate. Add additional seasonings to taste.

5. Serve cold or at room temperature.

Divine Design: Kidney Beans

If you're feeling soft around the middle, consider adding beans as a regular ingredient in your diet. When eaten without added sugar, beans help lower cholesterol and reduce body fat.

 ### Variations

- Top the salad with crumbled feta or goat cheese, sliced olives or diced avocado.

- Add a chopped carrot or a diced cucumber to the salad.

- Toss the dressing with lightly steamed asparagus, chopped red onion and white beans for a side dish or meatless main dish.

Mix and Match Salad

What's a vegetable chapter without a green salad recipe? Even though we only dedicate two pages to green salads (our other salad recipes focus on non-leafy veggies), we are not neglecting this healthy staple. Just top the greens of your choice with vegetables and a dressing. For additional taste and crunch, add your choice of pantry toppings, fruit and herbs. Adding a protein (or a combination of proteins) will turn your salad into a meal!

GREENS

Choose one or more greens as the foundation for your salad.

VEGETABLES AND FRUIT

These fresh vegetables (and fruits) can be diced or sliced according to your personal preference. We suggest cleaning them well and not peeling them (cucumbers, carrots, pears, etc.).

DRESSINGS

If you have the time, we suggest preparing homemade salad dressings; many of these will keep for several weeks. Otherwise look for commercial salad dressings with as few ingredients as possible.

PANTRY TOPPINGS

These yummy salad toppings keep well in your pantry and enhance your salads. While some are closer to God's design than others, if they help you eat more vegetables, it is probably a good thing!

FRESH HERBS

Fresh herbs can add unique flavors to your salads, and they are often packed with God-given antioxidants and other nutrients. A little goes a long way, so use them sparingly.

PROTEIN

Adding protein to your salad is an easy way to use leftovers or pantry items such as nuts, beans or seeds.

GREENS	VEGETABLES	DRESSINGS	PANTRY TOPPINGS	PROTEIN
Green leaf	Avocados	*Balsamic Vinaigrette* (page 23)	Artichoke hearts	Beans (canned), rinsed and drained (such as garbanzo, black or white beans)
Mesclun	Bell peppers	*Caesar Dressing* (page 26)	Capers	Crumbled cheese (feta, goat, mozzarella)
Red leaf	Broccoli	*Creamy Basil Dressing* (page 27)	Dried cranberries	Hard-boiled eggs, crumbled
Romaine	Cabbage	*Cucumber Dill Dressing* (page 28)	Hearts of palm	Cubed leftover *Basic Cooked Chicken* (page 74)
Spinach	Carrots	*Honey Mustard Dressing* (page 30)	Mandarin oranges	Nuts (such as walnuts, pecans or almonds)
	Cauliflower	Lemon juice, olive oil, dash of salt and pepper	Olives	Seeds (such as pumpkin, sunflower or sesame)
FRUIT	Celery	*Lemon Vinaigrette* (page 25)	Raisins	Tuna (canned), drained and flaked
Apples	Cucumbers	*Poppy Seed Dressing* (page 75)	Sesame sticks	
Mangoes	Onions (red, yellow or green)	*Ranch Dressing* (page 29)	Sun-dried tomatoes, rehydrated and diced	
Peaches	Peas	*Raspberry Vinaigrette* (page 24)	Water chestnuts	
Pears	Radishes	*Strawberry Dressing* (page 31)		
Pineapple	Tomatoes	Store-bought dressing of your choice	**FRESH HERBS**	
Strawberries	Zucchini		Cilantro	
			Basil	
			Dill	
			Mint	
			Parsley	

Cucumber Salad

Serve Cucumber Salad with *Asian Chicken* (page 78) or *Chicken with Peanut Sauce* (page 76).

Makes about 3 cups.

1 unpeeled large cucumber

¼ medium red onion

Juice of 2 limes (about 4 tablespoons)
1 tablespoon honey
½ teaspoon salt

1 cup firmly packed cilantro, mostly leaves

¼ cup peanuts

1. Cut the cucumber in half lengthwise, then in half again. Dice the strips into small pieces and put in a medium bowl. (Removing the seeds from the cucumber while it is still in long strips will help keep this salad fresh longer, but it is not necessary.)

2. Chop the onion and add to the bowl.

3. In a separate small bowl juice the limes and whisk in the honey and salt. Add to the cucumber mixture.

4. Finely chop the cilantro and add to the cucumber mixture.

5. Chop the peanuts and add to the cucumber mixture.

6. Mix the salad to incorporate the flavors.

Divine Design: Cucumbers

During the long, hot days of summer you may be looking for a cool fix for sunburns or tired, puffy eyes. The cucumber is naturally hydrating—made mostly of water—and its vitamin C and caffeic acid soothe and smooth the complexion. No wonder the Israelites yearned for them as they wandered the desert (Numbers 11:5).

Love Thy Leftovers

- This salad should be eaten within 2 days.

- Serve leftover Cucumber Salad as a side relish for *Basic Cooked Chicken* (page 74) or *Basic Cooked Fish* (page 63).

Cauliflower Salad with Sun-Dried Tomatoes and Olives

Makes 4 to 5 cups.

12 sun-dried tomatoes

1 small head of cauliflower

⅓ bunch parsley (mostly leaves)
½ cup pitted olives (green or black)
2 garlic cloves
2 tablespoons white wine vinegar
1 tablespoon extra virgin olive oil
¼ medium red onion
½ teaspoon salt
Several generous grindings of pepper

1. Add the sun-dried tomatoes to a small bowl and cover them with very hot tap water. Let stand for 10 to 15 minutes, or until soft. (If you are using oil-packed sun-dried tomatoes, there is no need to soak them; just shake off the excess oil before using.)

2. While the tomatoes rehydrate, cut or break the cauliflower into bite-sized florets and steam until they are barely tender, about 8 to 10 minutes.

3. Drain the sun-dried tomatoes and chop them into small pieces. Add to a food processor along with the remaining ingredients. Process until finely chopped (it will look like a thick, chunky paste).

4. In a large bowl combine the tomato mixture and cauliflower. Mix to incorporate, and serve warm or at room temperature.

Divine Design: Cauliflower

If you want to get the most out of these fabulous cancer-fighting florets, go natural. Boiling this vegetable throws nearly half of its nutrients down the drain. The best way to eat cauliflower is to grab it straight from God's kitchen—eat it raw or lightly steamed.

Variations

- Prepare the cauliflower as indicated, but instead of using the other ingredients listed, toss with *Olive and Sun-Dried Tomato Tapenade* (page 194).

- For a chunkier salad, chop the ingredients by hand rather than using the food processor.

Beet Salad

Makes about 4 cups.

2 large beets (or 1, 15-ounce can)

½ medium onion

2 tablespoons feta cheese (1 to 2 ounces)
2 tablespoons capers
1 tablespoon red wine vinegar
1 teaspoon extra virgin olive oil
1 teaspoon Dijon mustard
½ teaspoon dried dill
Scant ¼ teaspoon salt
Several generous grindings of pepper

1. Preheat the oven to 350 degrees. (If you are using canned beets, start at step 5.)

2. Cut off any green tops from the beets. (See Love Thy Leftovers for how to prepare these greens.) Wash, scrub and pat the beets dry.

3. Pierce the beets with a knife or fork (like you would before baking a potato), and individually wrap each beet in foil. Bake for 1 to 1½ hours, or until they are tender when pierced.

4. Once the beets have cooled, peel off the outer shell using a paring knife or vegetable peeler.

5. Cut the beets into ¼- to ½-inch pieces and place in a bowl.

6. Chop the onion and add to the bowl.

7. Add the remaining ingredients to the bowl and combine, coating the vegetables.

8. Serve the salad chilled or at room temperature.

 Divine Design: Beets

Beet juice is a potent weapon against the cell mutations caused by cancer-causing nitrates. Nitrates are most often found in processed meats (such as hot dogs and bologna), where they are used as chemical preservatives. So avoid unhealthy, processed meats and eat God's juicy beets.

Love Thy Leftovers

Don't throw away those beet greens! Use them as a substitute for chard in *Swiss Chard with Pine Nuts and Golden Raisins* (page 18), or simply sauté them in olive oil and add salt, pepper and balsamic vinegar to taste.

Basic Roasted Vegetables

Makes 2 to 3 servings.

1 pound mixed vegetables, such as:
- ☉ Red, yellow or orange bell peppers
- ☉ Onions (any color)
- ☉ Zucchini or yellow squash
- ☉ Eggplant
- ☉ Garlic cloves

1 tablespoon extra virgin olive oil

Several dashes of salt

Several generous grindings of pepper

1 teaspoon dried herbs (any combination of dried basil, oregano, thyme, rosemary; optional)

1. Preheat the oven to 400 degrees.

2. Cut the vegetables into uniform pieces so they cook evenly, and add to a large bowl with the remaining ingredients. Toss to completely coat the vegetables.

3. Transfer the vegetables to a jelly roll pan (or cookie sheet), spread in an even layer, and bake for 20 minutes.

4. Stir the vegetables and return to the oven. Check the vegetables every 10 minutes or so. Depending on the size and type of your vegetables, the total cooking time will range from 30 to 45 minutes. They are done when they turn golden brown and are easily pierced with a fork.

Divine Design: Vegetables

When you follow God's design for eating, it shows. The Israelite prophet Daniel was offered food from the Babylonian king's table. Rather than go against God's design, he and his three friends asked to eat only vegetables. After only ten days, they were noticeably healthier and better nourished than anyone else!

Variations

- ☉ For roasted root vegetables, use any combination of carrots, sweet potatoes, turnips, parsnips and celery root.

- ☉ Add cherry tomatoes to the pan during the last 20 minutes of cooking.

- ☉ For a roasted vegetable salad, allow the vegetables to cool and toss with balsamic vinegar and additional salt and pepper to taste.

- ☉ To grill the vegetables, follow step 2, making sure to cut the vegetables into large chunks. On an oiled grill over medium-low heat, grill for 3 to 5 minutes per side, or until the vegetables reach the desired doneness.

- ☉ Sauté the vegetables on the stovetop over medium-high heat until they reach the desired doneness.

Love Thy Leftovers

- ☉ For a tasty rice salad, toss the leftover vegetables with *Basic Cooked Rice* (page 39) and the salad dressing of your choice.

- ☉ Add the leftover vegetables to *Quesadillas* (page 111), *Refried Bean Wraps* (page 105), *Mix and Match Salad* (page 10) or *Mix and Match Whole Grain Pasta* (page 46).

Maple Walnut Acorn Squash

Makes 2 squash halves.

1 medium acorn squash

---

1 cup walnuts
½ cup raisins
¼ cup dried unsweetened coconut
1 tablespoon maple syrup
½ teaspoon vanilla

1. Preheat the oven to 350 degrees.

2. Cut the squash in half, across the middle.

3. Scoop out the seeds and any stringy stuff. (If you want to eat the seeds, see the variation to *Cajun-Spiced Pumpkin Seeds*, page 200.)

4. Put the squash halves in an 8 x 8-inch baking pan with the cut side facing up.

5. In a food processor or a blender, combine the remaining ingredients and pulse until the nuts and raisins are coarsely chopped. Scoop the walnut mixture into the squash halves.

6. Fill the bottom of the pan with water ¼ to ½ inch high. Loosely cover the pan with foil and bake for about 1 hour, or until the squash flesh is very tender.

7. Eat the squash directly out of the shell, cut the shell into pieces, or scoop the squash and filling into a large bowl and mix together.

Divine Design: Acorn Squash

The acorn squash certainly lives up to its name. The many nutrients in this winter variety (including beta-carotene, potassium, vitamin A, vitamin C, fiber and folic acid) all help "squash" health problems such as colon cancer, heart disease, birth defects, emphysema and lung cancer.

 Variations

⊕ Substitute pecans for the walnuts.

⊕ Experiment with different dried fruits, such as apricots or dates.

⊕ Use butternut squash instead of acorn squash. Remove the "neck" and fill the remaining squash cavity with the prepared filling.

 Love Thy Leftovers

⊕ Reheat the leftovers for breakfast.

⊕ Use any leftover filling as a topping on yogurt, or serve on *Hot Millet Cereal* (page 150), *Creamy Brown Rice Cereal* (page 151) or *Hot Oat Cereal* (page 149).

Roasted Asparagus

Makes 4 servings.

1 bunch asparagus (about 1 pound)

1 tablespoon extra virgin olive oil
Several dashes of salt
Several generous grindings of pepper
2 finely chopped garlic cloves (optional)

2 teaspoons Parmesan cheese (optional)
Juice of ¼ lemon (about 1 tablespoon;
    optional)

1. Preheat the oven to 400 degrees.

2. Break off the tough ends from the asparagus (the woody inch or so at the bottom of each stalk). Place the asparagus in a shallow baking or jelly roll pan (not a cookie sheet).

3. Add olive oil, salt, pepper and garlic (if using) to the pan, toss, and arrange the asparagus in a single layer in the pan.

5. Bake for about 10 minutes.

6. Remove the pan from the oven and gently toss the asparagus. If using, add the cheese and lemon juice.

7. Return the pan to the oven and continue cooking until the asparagus reaches the desired consistency and begins to brown slightly, about 4 to 8 minutes. The cooking time will vary, depending on the thickness of the stalks and whether you prefer your asparagus crisp or soft.

Divine Design: Asparagus

A little goes a long way with this healthy vegetable. Your body uses God-designed folates to battle heart disease, and asparagus is packed with them. Just one serving of this stalk provides nearly 60 percent of the daily recommended intake of folates.

 ## Variation

Grill the asparagus instead of baking it.

Swiss Chard with Pine Nuts and Golden Raisins

Makes about 1½ cups.

1 large bunch red or green Swiss chard
(about 5 stalks)

1 to 2 garlic cloves

⅓ cup golden raisins (or dark raisins)
¼ cup pine nuts
1 to 2 tablespoons extra virgin olive oil

Several dashes of salt
Several generous grindings of pepper

1. Wash the chard and cut off and discard the stems and the thick rib from the leaves. Leave some moisture on the leaves; it will be used to steam the chard. Cut the leaves into bite-sized pieces.

2. Finely chop the garlic.

3. In a frying pan sauté the garlic, raisins and pine nuts in the olive oil over medium heat until the raisins begin to soften, about 5 minutes.

4. Add the chard to the pan and sauté, stirring frequently, until it begins to soften or until the greens are wilted, about 5 minutes. Add salt and pepper to taste.

Divine Design: Swiss Chard

Are dairy products the only way to strong bones? Not according to God's menu. A one-cup serving of chard will give you 10 percent of the calcium and 34 percent of the magnesium you need every day to keep your bones healthy for life.

 Variations

⊙ Use kale or the tops of beets instead of the chard.

⊙ Experiment with different dried fruit and nuts, such as cranberries and walnuts, instead of the raisins and pine nuts.

⊙ Use a thinly sliced leek instead of or in addition to the garlic.

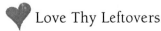 Love Thy Leftovers

Did you know that the chard stems are edible? Instead of throwing them away, dice them and sauté them in olive oil. Add salt, pepper or other seasonings to taste.

Garlic Ginger Broccoli

Makes about 4 cups.

1 bunch broccoli (about 1 pound without the stalks)

1-inch piece of fresh ginger
3 to 4 garlic cloves

2 tablespoons extra virgin olive oil
Juice of ¼ lemon (about 1 tablespoon)
Dash of cayenne pepper
Scant ¼ teaspoon salt
Several generous grindings of pepper

1. Preheat the oven to 400 degrees and oil a jelly roll pan or cookie sheet.

2. Remove the broccoli stems and break or cut the florets into bite-sized pieces. Place them in a medium bowl.

3. Peel the ginger and grate or finely chop it. Chop the garlic. Add both to the bowl.

4. Add the remaining ingredients to the bowl and mix to coat the broccoli.

5. Spread the broccoli onto the prepared pan and bake for 15 to 20 minutes (15 minutes for crunchier broccoli and 20 minutes for softer broccoli).

Divine Design: Ginger

This natural medication comes straight from the Creator. Adding ginger to your diet helps soothe arthritis pain by prohibiting blood vessel inflammation. And if you are prone to motion sickness, a small dose of ginger will help calm your tummy.

 Variations

Instead of baking the broccoli, stir-fry over medium-high heat for 4 to 7 minutes, or until it reaches the desired doneness.

Love Thy Leftovers

Grate the unused broccoli stalks into a salad, use them for *Broccoli Peanut Slaw* (page 6) or *Classic Coleslaw* (page 5), or sauté them as you would any other vegetable.

Spaghetti Squash

We often add a protein such as chicken or white beans to spaghetti squash, so we end up with a main dish (see the variations).

1 medium spaghetti squash

Marinara Sauce (page 32) or store-bought pasta sauce

Parmesan cheese (optional)

1. Preheat the oven to 350 degrees.

2. Using a large knife, cut the squash in half, across the width. Scoop out the seeds. (If you want to eat the seeds, see the variation to *Cajun-Spiced Pumpkin Seeds,* page 200).

3. Place the squash halves flesh side down on an 8 x 8- or 9 x 13-inch baking pan. Add ¼ inch of water to the bottom of the pan.

4. Bake the squash for 45 to 60 minutes. You will know it is done when you press on the outside of the squash and it has softened.

5. Allow the squash to cool for several minutes. During this time heat the pasta sauce in a medium saucepan over medium heat.

6. Once the squash has cooled slightly, scoop out the insides. They will pull out easily and look like strands of spaghetti. If the strands look soggy, squeeze out the excess liquid with paper towels or a clean dishtowel.

7. Place the squash in individual serving bowls and top with the sauce and Parmesan cheese (if using).

Divine Design: Spaghetti Squash

God knew how much you'd love eating spaghetti, so He created spaghetti squash—a vegetable that you could use as a pasta alternative. While the taste and texture are not identical to man-made pasta, the God-made pasta, when paired with a delicious sauce, is healthier and just as satisfying.

Variations

⊙ For a main dish, add *Turkey Sausage* (page 86) or a 15-ounce can of white beans, or use *Old-Fashioned Meat Sauce* (page 90) instead of sauce.

⊙ Use cooked spaghetti squash in place of millet in *Millet Casserole* (page 49).

⊙ Instead of baking the squash halves, place them in a steamer and steam until tender.

Sweet Potato Fries

Makes about 3 servings.

1 unpeeled medium sweet potato (about 1 pound)

2 tablespoons extra virgin olive oil
1 heaping teaspoon ground cumin
¼ to ½ teaspoon salt
Several generous grindings of pepper

1. Preheat the oven to 400 degrees.

2. Cut the sweet potatoes into strips, so they look like french fries.

3. Put the sweet potatoes, olive oil, cumin, salt and pepper in a large bowl and toss to completely coat. Transfer the sweet potatoes to a jelly roll pan (or a cookie sheet) and spread in an even layer.

4. Bake for 15 minutes, gently stir with a rubber spatula or wooden spoon, and return to the oven.

5. Cook for an additional 15 minutes. Depending on the size of your "french fries," the total cooking time will range from 30 to 40 minutes. They are done when they turn golden brown and are easily pierced with a fork.

Divine Design: Sweet Potatoes

Like carrots, bright orange sweet potatoes were created by God to be filled with beta-carotene, which helps prevent cataracts. That's why they're both "good for the eyes."

Variations

- Add ½ teaspoon chili powder during step 3.

- Experiment with different spice mixtures. For example, substitute 1 teaspoon dried thyme and 1 teaspoon dried rosemary for the cumin.

- Use 4 large carrots instead of the sweet potatoes.

- Cut a medium zucchini into the same-sized pieces as the sweet potato and add during step 3.

Love Thy Leftovers

Dice leftover Sweet Potato Fries and add to *Basic Scrambled Eggs* (page 152).

Sweet Potato Casserole

This is the sweetest "vegetable" dish you'll ever eat!

Makes 6 servings.

1½ pounds unpeeled sweet potatoes (about 2 medium)

1 large zucchini

⅔ to 1 cup walnuts

⅔ to 1 cup raisins

¼ cup apple juice or water
Heaping ¼ teaspoon salt
½ teaspoon cinnamon
Splash of extra virgin olive oil
Splash of maple syrup

1. Preheat the oven to 350 degrees.

2. Thinly slice the sweet potatoes and zucchini.

3. Chop the walnuts.

4. Layer the casserole ingredients in an 8 x 8-inch baking pan in the following order:

   a. ⅓ of the sweet potato slices

   b. ½ of the raisins

   c. ½ of the nuts

   d. ½ of the zucchini slices

   e. ⅓ of the sweet potato slices

   f. Remainder of the raisins and nuts

   g. Remainder of the zucchini slices

   h. Remainder of the sweet potato slices

5. Whisk together the remaining ingredients in a small bowl and pour over the top of the casserole.

6. Cover the pan with foil and bake for about 1 hour. The casserole is done when the vegetables are very tender.

 Variations

Substitute 2 apples for the zucchini.

Balsamic Vinaigrette

Makes about 1 cup.

2 garlic cloves

¼ cup balsamic vinegar

1 heaping tablespoon Dijon mustard

1 tablespoon honey

1 teaspoon dried dill (or 3 or 4 sprigs of fresh dill)

⅔ cup extra virgin olive oil

1. Finely chop the garlic using a food processor or blender.

2. Combine the vinegar, mustard, honey and dill in the blender. Process until everything is finely chopped.

3. While the food processor is running, slowly pour the olive oil through the feed tube and blend until smooth.

 Divine Design: Olive Oil

The fats from olive oil are good for you. God placed these monounsaturated fatty acids in olives to help remove bad cholesterol from your body.

Variations

⊙ Experiment with different kinds of balsamic vinegars, such as pear or fig.

⊙ Experiment with different kinds of vinegars, such as white wine.

Raspberry Vinaigrette

Makes about 1 cup.

¼ medium red onion

¼ cup white wine vinegar
¼ cup raspberry all-fruit spread
½ teaspoon salt
½ teaspoon celery seed

½ cup extra virgin olive oil

1. Finely chop the onion using a food processor or blender.

2. Add the vinegar, all-fruit spread, salt and celery seed, and blend to combine.

3. While the food processor is running, slowly pour the olive oil through the feed tube and blend until smooth.

 Variations

Experiment with different all-fruit spreads, such as apricot or strawberry.

Lemon Vinaigrette

In addition to a salad dressing, Lemon Vinaigrette makes a great marinade for fish or chicken, or a tasty dressing to toss with pasta salad.

Makes about 1 cup.

1 to 2 garlic cloves

Juice of ¾ lemon (about 3 tablespoons)
2 tablespoons Dijon mustard
3 tablespoons red wine vinegar
1 tablespoon honey
1 teaspoon dried oregano
Heaping ¼ teaspoon salt
Several generous grindings of pepper
½ cup extra virgin olive oil

1. Finely mince the garlic cloves.

2. Combine the garlic with the remaining ingredients in a small glass jar and shake well, or whisk together in a small bowl.

 Divine Design: Lemons

When God gives you lemons, rejoice! Both the juice and the zest are loaded with health-promoting vitamin C, which helps protect your body against cancer, fights off cold symptoms and helps heal cuts and bruises.

 Variation

For lemon-basil dressing, add a few chopped fresh basil leaves during step 2.

Love Thy Leftovers

Use ¼ cup Lemon Vinaigrette in place of the dressing for *Rice Salad Primavera* (page 40), or use ½ cup in place of the dressing for *Barley Veggie Salad* (page 45).

Caesar Dressing

Caesar dressing is typically made with anchovies—one of God's healthiest fish. We have included anchovies in our recipe, but feel free to use less than the amount indicated or omit them altogether.

Makes about 1 cup.

2 garlic cloves

---

6 tablespoons extra virgin olive oil

Juice of 1½ lemons (about 6 tablespoons)

2 tablespoons Worcestershire sauce

¼ cup mayonnaise

¼ cup Parmesan cheese

Several generous grindings of pepper

Heaping ¼ teaspoon salt

½ of a 2-ounce can of flat anchovy fillets packed in oil, undrained

1. Chop the garlic in a blender or food processor.

2. Add the remaining ingredients to the blender and blend until smooth.

 Divine Design: Garlic

Stimulate and protect your immune system with this natural antibiotic. Unlike many synthetic antibiotics that lose potency when dangerous bacteria become resistant, God's natural cures still stand up for your health and wellness.

♥ Love Thy Leftovers

Use leftover anchovy filets in a *Mix and Match Salad* (page 10) or on *Polenta Pizza* (page 52).

Creamy Basil Dressing

This dressing makes a good topping for baked potatoes or either version of *Veggie Burgers* (pages 108 and 109).

Makes about 1 cup.

½ cup plain yogurt
Juice of 1 lemon (about ¼ cup)
1 to 2 garlic cloves
12 fresh basil leaves
½ teaspoon dried thyme
½ teaspoon dried dill
Several dashes of salt
Several generous grindings of pepper

⅓ cup extra virgin olive oil

1. Combine all of the ingredients (except the olive oil) in a food processor or blender. Blend until well incorporated.

2. While the food processor is running, slowly pour the oil though the feed tube and blend until smooth.

 Divine Design: Basil

The bacteria strains that cause boils, toxic shock syndrome, urinary tract infections and pneumonia are rapidly evolving toward resistance to all known antibiotics. So what's the big deal about basil? God created basil to fight against these harmful strains and protect your body naturally. Unlike the antibiotics that have failed, God's creation still succeeds.

Variations

For a thicker dressing, add up to ½ zucchini and/or 3 green onions during step 1.

Cucumber Dill Dressing

This dressing makes a good topping for *Gyros* (page 88).

Makes about 1 cup.

⅛ medium onion
¼ unpeeled medium cucumber

¼ cup plain yogurt
¼ cup mayonnaise
Juice of ½ lemon (about 2 tablespoons)
Heaping ¼ teaspoon salt
Heaping ¼ teaspoon dried dill (or 1 sprig of
   fresh dill)

1. Add the onion and cucumber to a blender or food processor and blend until chopped.

2. Add the remaining ingredients and blend until smooth.

Divine Design: Dill

This flavorful plant may be light and wispy in appearance, but it helps keep bones strong with generous amounts of calcium, iron and magnesium—important nutrients God provided to help prevent bone loss.

 ## Variations

⊛ Add several pieces of feta cheese during step 1.

⊛ Experiment with different proportions of yogurt and mayonnaise.

⊛ Experiment with different fresh herbs, such as cilantro or mint.

 ## Love Thy Leftovers

Cucumber Dill Dressing is best used within 3 or 4 days.

Ranch Dressing or Dip

Besides a salad dressing or vegetable dip, Ranch Dressing can be used to top baked potatoes or either version of *Veggie Burgers* (pages 108 and 109). It's also great as a sandwich spread or as a dipping sauce for *Basic Cooked Chicken* (page 74).

Makes about 1½ cups.

¼ onion
1 garlic clove

½ cup mayonnaise
½ cup plain yogurt or kefir
Scant ¼ teaspoon salt
2 teaspoons dried parsley
2 teaspoons apple cider vinegar
Several generous grindings of pepper

1. Finely chop the onion and garlic in a blender or food processor.
2. Add the remaining ingredients and blend until smooth.

Divine Design: Yogurt

Yogurt isn't just a tasty breakfast food. Protecting your body from influenza, dysentery, and salmonella and staph poisoning, this dairy product is a natural antibiotic.

 Variations

- Experiment with different proportions of yogurt and mayonnaise.
- Use 2 tablespoons chopped fresh parsley (or other fresh herbs) in place of the dried.
- Substitute 2 teaspoons onion powder or onion flakes and ½ teaspoon garlic powder for the fresh onion and garlic.

Honey Mustard Dressing

Serve Honey Mustard Dressing over a spinach salad or other salad of your choice.

Makes about ¾ cup.

2 tablespoons extra virgin olive oil

¼ cup honey

¼ cup Dijon mustard

¼ cup apple cider vinegar

Several dashes of salt

Several generous grindings of pepper

1. Combine all of the ingredients in a small glass jar and shake well, or whisk together in a small bowl.

Divine Design: Honey

Honey contains important nutrients, so God made it tasty to entice you to eat it. Honey has 165 ingredients, including 18 amino acids and assorted minerals and enzymes—none of which are contained in refined sugar. Two of these ingredients are proline (good for the bones) and calcium. Proverbs 16:24 says, "Pleasant words are a honeycomb, sweet to the soul *and healing to the bones*." (emphasis added)

Variations

⊙ For French dressing, substitute 2 tablespoons tomato paste for the mustard and reduce the honey to 3 tablespoons.

⊙ Substitute maple syrup for the honey.

Strawberry Dressing

Makes about 1 cup.

1 cup sliced fresh strawberries

3 tablespoons balsamic vinegar

1 tablespoon orange juice or apple juice

1 tablespoon extra virgin olive oil

Heaping ¼ teaspoon dried thyme

1 teaspoon Dijon mustard

Several dashes of salt

Several generous grindings of pepper

1. Combine all of the ingredients in a blender or food processor. Blend until smooth.

 Divine Design: Strawberries

Strawberries are one of the best health investments on the shelf. Their divine design contains more "bang for the buck" than most other fruits—their antioxidants fight free radicals that can cause vision loss, cancer growth and heart disease.

 Variations

⊛ Use thawed frozen strawberries instead of fresh.

⊛ Experiment with different types of berries, such as raspberries or blueberries.

♥ Love Thy Leftovers

Strawberry Dressing stays fresh for 2 or 3 days in the refrigerator.

Marinara Sauce

Makes about 3 quarts.

1 large onion

6 to 10 garlic cloves

Extra virgin olive oil

10 cups chopped tomatoes (choose one):
- 12 to 15 medium tomatoes, chopped
- 20 to 30 plum tomatoes, chopped
- 3, 28-ounce cans of chopped tomatoes, undrained

1½ teaspoons salt

1 teaspoon dried oregano

1 teaspoon dried basil

Several generous grindings of pepper

1, 6-ounce can of tomato paste

¾ cup wine (red or white)

1. Chop the onion and garlic.

2. Coat the bottom of a large stockpot with olive oil (about 2 tablespoons), and sauté the onion and garlic over medium-high heat until the onions are soft, about 5 to 10 minutes.

3. Add the tomatoes, spices and tomato paste to the pot and simmer, partially covered, for about 1 hour.

4. Add the wine to the pot and simmer for an additional 30 minutes.

5. Ladle the sauce into a blender and puree in several batches.

6. Pour the puree back into the stockpot, heat through, and serve.

Divine Design: Red Wine

Red wine's well-publicized health benefits come from the powerful antioxidants found in grape skins and seeds. These intelligently designed weapons fight cancer and heart disease, and they might even prevent signs of aging. While the Bible clearly cautions against drinking too much wine, many of wine's nearly 250 appearances in the Bible were approved by God and even encouraged.

 ## Love Thy Leftovers

- Marina Sauce freezes very well. Freeze any leftover sauce in an airtight plastic container or a freezer bag, and thaw before using.

- Use the sauce for *Millet Casserole* (page 49), *Spaghetti Squash* (page 20) or *Polenta Pizza* (page 52).

 ## Variations

- For a chunkier sauce, don't add the sauce to the blender (skip steps 5 and 6).

- Use 1 tablespoon fresh herbs instead of dried. Stir into the sauce during step 4.

Pesto

Toss pesto with pasta, rice or roasted vegetables, or use it as a sandwich spread. It can also be used with *Mix and Match Whole Grain Pasta* (page 46) or *Polenta Pizza* (page 52).

Makes about 2 cups.

3 cups firmly packed fresh basil leaves

3 garlic cloves

¼ to ⅓ cup pine nuts or walnuts
⅓ to ½ cup Parmesan cheese
¼ to ¾ teaspoon salt
Several generous grindings of pepper

½ cup extra virgin olive oil

1. Trim off the stems from the basil.

2. Finely chop the garlic using a food processor.

3. Combine the basil, garlic and all of the remaining ingredients (except the olive oil) in the food processor. Process until everything is finely chopped.

4. While the food processor is running, slowly pour the olive oil through the feed tube. Process until smooth.

5. If needed, add additional salt and pepper.

 Variations

☺ Rehydrate ⅓ cup sun-dried tomatoes and add to step 3.

☺ Experiment with fresh herbs. For example, use ⅔ bunch fresh parsley instead of 1 to 2 cups of the basil.

☺ Substitute a bunch of kale or Swiss chard for the basil, increase the number of garlic cloves to 5, and add the juice of 1 lemon (about ¼ cup). The remaining ingredients stay the same.

 Love Thy Leftovers

☺ Pesto freezes well. Freeze in ice cube trays or other small containers, and thaw before using.

☺ Spread pesto over fish and cook according to the directions in *Pesto-Crusted Salmon* (page 65), or spread over chicken breasts and cook according to the directions in *Basic Cooked Chicken* (page 74).

☺ Use as a dipping sauce with *Basic Cooked Chicken* (page 74) or *Basic Cooked Fish* (page 63).

Tomato Basil Vegetable Sauce

Serve over steamed or roasted asparagus, broccoli or other vegetables, or use it to top *Basic Cooked Rice* (page 39), *Basic Cooked Fish* (page 63) or a baked potato.

Makes about 2 cups.

1 red bell pepper
1 large tomato

¼ small onion
1 garlic clove

¼ cup extra virgin olive oil
Juice of ¼ lemon (about 1 tablespoon)
15 fresh basil leaves
Heaping ¼ teaspoon salt
Several generous grindings of pepper

1. Seed and quarter the pepper and remove the stem end from the tomato.

2. Combine the pepper and tomato with the onion and garlic in a blender or food processor and puree.

3. Add the remaining ingredients and puree until smooth. Serve at room temperature, or heat in a small saucepan before serving.

Divine Design: Tomatoes

These fruits may pose as vegetables, but more importantly, they pose a threat to prostate problems in men. The powerful beta-carotene, gamma-carotene, and provitamin A compounds God placed in tomatoes work together to prevent these difficulties.

 Variations

◉ Use the sauce for *Polenta Pizza* (page 52).

◉ Spread the sauce over chicken breasts or fish, and cook according to the directions for *Basic Cooked Chicken* (page 74) or *Pesto-Crusted Salmon* (page 65).

◉ Roast the pepper, tomato, onion and garlic according to the directions for *Basic Roasted Vegetables* (page 15) before pureeing.

Chapter 2
Grains and Potatoes

Like vegetables, grains were given to Adam "in the beginning," and they are also some of God's most carefully crafted foods. Think about it: They grow everywhere in the world, in any climate, and reproduce quickly. They have a long storage life (kernels found in Egyptian tombs can still be sprouted after four thousand years). And—if they are not processed or refined—grains meet nearly all of your nutritional needs, since they're filled with vitamins, minerals, fiber and even protein.

What kinds of grains are we talking about? You are probably familiar with brown rice or barley. Others, such as millet and quinoa, are less well-known but are gaining popularity. Potatoes and corn are technically vegetables, but they are good sources of complex carbohydrates if you're not in the mood for whole grains. When using potatoes, make sure to keep the skin on—that's where God put the fiber.

Other whole grains include wheat, buckwheat and spelt. We use these grains in their ground-up form (flour or pasta), so you generally will not find these grains in this chapter. (Flours made with these grains appear in other chapters, especially "Breakfast" and "Desserts and Fruit.")

You will notice two characteristics of our grain recipes. First, we use dressings and other flavor enhancements sparingly. For example, both *Barley Veggie Salad* and *Rice Salad Primavera* use very light dressings to highlight the grain's flavor, not cover it up. *Mashed Potatoes with a Twist* uses garlic and sweet potatoes to add flavor, rather than excessive butter and milk. And because individual preferences vary, we often encourage you to decide how much salt to use ("¼ to ½ teaspoon" or "several dashes of salt"). Do not be afraid to add salt to recipes that only use natural ingredients—God created salt to enhance food for your enjoyment. Like anything else, though, salt should be used in moderation.

We often add vegetables to our grain dishes. As we confessed in the last chapter, we never eat enough vegetables. By adding them to our grain dishes, we not only sneak them into our diets, but we also add a variety of flavors and colors to these grains.

If you are not used to eating whole grains, you might have to transition your taste buds and digestive system. For example, brown rice will taste nuttier and heavier than white rice because white rice has had several layers of nutrients—and taste—stripped away. We think you will enjoy the whole grain flavors, but if they are different from the flavors you are used to, be ready for a change!

Principle 1

God created an abundance of grains. The "seed-bearing plants" referred to in Genesis 1:29 include them all, whether they are millet and quinoa, or brown rice and barley.

Principle 2

Keep your grains whole. That is how God made them, and that is what is best for your body. And choosing organic whole grains will help you avoid man-made pesticides and genetically modified organisms (GMOs) that are harmful to your body.

Principle 3

The more whole grains and the fewer processed grains you eat (Principle 2), the more satisfied you will feel and the less likely you will be to overeat.

Basic Cooked Rice

If you do not have one, we highly recommend buying a rice cooker/vegetable steamer combination. It makes cooking rice a breeze!

Makes 3 cups.

1 cup brown rice

2 cups chicken or vegetable broth

OPTIONAL SEASONINGS (USE
  APPROXIMATELY 1 TEASPOON)

⊙ Combination of dried parsley, basil and/or oregano

⊙ Dried dill or ground cumin

1. Add the rice, broth and any optional seasonings to a medium saucepan. Bring the mixture to a boil over medium-high heat.

2. Reduce the heat to low, cover the pan with a tightly fitting lid, and simmer for 45 minutes.

3. After 45 minutes, turn off the flame and let the rice sit for about 10 minutes, without removing the cover. Fluff the rice with a fork before serving.

4. If you're using a rice cooker, adjust the liquid and cooking time according to your equipment's directions.

Divine Design: Rice

In its original God-given state, brown rice is filled with fiber. This helps relieve constipation, prevent a myriad of cancers and reduce the chance of diabetes. Remember, if it doesn't say "brown rice," it's probably not and it's not as nutritious as God-given brown rice.

Variations

⊙ Add a small chopped onion, chopped garlic and/or dried fruit (such as raisins) at the beginning of the cooking process.

⊙ Stir in chopped nuts, Parmesan cheese, and/or a tablespoon of butter before serving.

⊙ Substitute up to 2 cups tomato or vegetable juice for the broth, or up to ½ cup white wine for the broth.

Love Thy Leftovers

⊙ For a cold salad, toss leftover rice with leftover *Basic Roasted Vegetables* (page 15), leftover *Basic Cooked Chicken* (page 74) and a dash of balsamic vinegar and olive oil.

⊙ For a hot meal, stir-fry leftover rice with *Basic Cooked Fish* (page 63), chopped raw vegetables and olive oil.

⊙ Add leftover rice to most recipes from "Soup, Stew and Chili."

⊙ Toss leftover rice with dressing from *Green Bean and Tomato Salad with Garlic Basil Dressing* (page 8) or 2 to 3 tablespoons *Pesto* (page 33).

⊙ Use leftover unseasoned rice to make *Fried Rice* (page 99), *Tabbouleh Rice* (page 42) or *Quiche* (page 113).

Rice Salad Primavera

Makes 6 cups.

RICE
1 cup brown rice
2 cups chicken or vegetable broth

DRESSING
¼ teaspoon dried rosemary
1 garlic clove
2 tablespoons extra virgin olive oil
Juice of ½ lemon (about 2 tablespoons)
½ teaspoon dried oregano
¼ teaspoon salt
Several generous grindings of pepper

3 cups mixed, chopped vegetables, such as:
- Unpeeled carrots
- Onions
- Zucchini
- Red or green bell peppers
- Grape or cherry tomatoes
- Baby spinach

1. Prepare the rice with the broth according to the directions for *Basic Cooked Rice* (page 39), omitting the optional seasonings.

2. While the rice is cooking:

   a. Finely mince or crush the rosemary and garlic. Combine with the remaining dressing ingredients in a small glass jar and shake well, or whisk together in a small bowl.

   b. Dice the carrots, onions, zucchini and peppers; halve the tomatoes; and shred the spinach into thin strips.

3. When the rice is done, transfer it to a large bowl. Add the dressing and toss lightly.

4. Add the vegetables and toss again. Add additional salt to taste. Serve at room temperature.

 Divine Design: Rice

The health benefits God put into brown rice can be enjoyed by those who are sensitive to gluten-filled grains, such as wheat. Brown rice is easy to digest and is gluten free.

 Variations

- Experiment with different combinations of other vegetables.
- Use *Basic Roasted Vegetables* (page 15) instead of raw vegetables.
- Experiment with different whole grains (such as barley) instead of rice.
- Use bottled dressing instead of making your own.

Love Thy Leftovers

Add leftover rice salad to any tossed green salad.

Wild Rice Pilaf Salad

We suggest using a ready-made wild rice mix, such as Lundberg's Wild Blend.

Makes about 6 cups.

1 cup wild rice/brown rice mix
2 to 2½ cups chicken or vegetable broth

1 unpeeled carrot
1 celery stalk
½ medium onion or 3 green onions (white part and some green)
½ cup pecans, almonds or walnuts

½ cup dried cranberries or cherries
¼ cup dried golden (or dark) raisins
¼ cup sunflower seeds
½ cup frozen peas
¼ to ½ teaspoon salt
Several generous grindings of pepper

1. Add the rice and broth to a medium saucepan. (Adjust the amount of broth according to package instructions.) Bring the rice to a boil over medium-high heat.

2. Reduce the heat to low, cover the pan with a tightly fitting lid, and simmer for about 45 to 55 minutes. (Adjust the simmer time according to package instructions.)

3. While the rice cooks, finely dice the carrots, celery and onion, and coarsely chop the nuts.

4. Combine the rice with the chopped vegetables, chopped nuts and remaining ingredients, and mix to incorporate. Serve warm or at room temperature.

Divine Design: Wild Rice

Wild rice—which is actually a grass, not a grain—is native to North America and is an excellent source of minerals. It's also higher in protein than other rice varieties.

 ### Variations

⊛ Experiment by using different whole grains (such as wheat berries) instead of the rice blend.

⊛ Toss the rice salad with 1 tablespoon *Balsamic Vinaigrette* (page 23).

⊛ Add ½ apple, finely diced, to the rice salad.

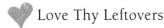 ### Love Thy Leftovers

Toss leftover rice salad with cubes of *Basic Cooked Chicken* (page 74); serve hot or cold.

Tabbouleh Rice

This makes a delicious topping or side dish for *Gyros* (page 88).

Makes about 2 cups.

⅔ bunch parsley (mostly leaves)

2 sprigs of fresh mint (about 15 to 20 leaves)

1 small onion or 2 to 3 green onions (white part and some green)

1 large tomato (or 1 cup grape or cherry tomatoes)

Juice of 1 lemon (about ¼ cup)

2 to 3 tablespoons extra virgin olive oil

1 cup cooked brown rice (see *Basic Cooked Rice*, page 39)

¼ to ½ teaspoon salt

Several generous grindings of pepper

1. Finely chop the parsley, mint and onion, and add to a small bowl.

2. Cut the tomato into bite-sized pieces, or halve the grape tomatoes. Add to the bowl.

3. Mix the chopped vegetables and herbs with the remaining ingredients. Adjust any ingredients to taste.

4. If time permits, refrigerate about 1 hour before serving.

 Divine Design: Parsley

Fruits aren't the only foods God provided to help ward off cold symptoms. Parsley is filled with vitamin C that can make the cold virus much more bearable, and perhaps even prevent colds from the start.

💜 Love Thy Leftovers

Add cooked lentils from *Lentil Salad* (page 104) to leftover Tabbouleh Rice. Add additional salt, pepper, lemon juice or other ingredients to taste.

Spinach and Cilantro Green Rice

Serve with *Halibut with Salsa* (page 70) or *Vegetable Chili* (page 135).

Makes about 5 cups.

⅔ bunch cilantro (stems OK)

1 cup firmly packed fresh spinach
1¼ cups milk or rice milk
1¼ cups chicken or vegetable broth
Juice of ½ lime (about 1 tablespoon)

1½ cups brown rice
Heaping ½ teaspoon salt
Several generous grindings of pepper

1. Trim the cilantro stems 1 to 2 inches.

2. Add the cilantro, spinach, milk, broth and lime juice to a blender and puree the ingredients. (If you are using a food processor, do this in two batches.)

3. Combine the liquid mixture with the remaining ingredients in a medium saucepan. Bring the mixture to a boil over medium-high heat.

4. Reduce the heat to low, cover the pan with a tightly fitting lid, and simmer for 45 minutes.

5. After 45 minutes, turn off the flame and let the rice sit for about 10 minutes, without removing the cover. Fluff the rice with a fork before serving.

 Divine Design: Spinach and Cilantro

Both spinach and cilantro contain chlorophyll, the ingredient that puts the "green" in "green leafy vegetables" and that God created to cleanse and detoxify your body.

 Variations

⊚ Add a chopped small onion and 2 minced garlic cloves to the saucepan during step 3.

⊚ Experiment by adding ground cumin and chili powder along with the other seasonings.

⊚ Substitute parsley for the cilantro.

♥ Love Thy Leftovers

⊚ For a whole wheat tortilla filling, mix leftover green rice with beans or *Basic Cooked Chicken* (page 74).

⊚ Reheat leftover green rice with a little broth or water to moisten it; for added flavor, add *Pesto* (page 33) or a little butter.

Barley "Risotto"

This recipe takes a while to cook, but it's worth the time. It doesn't need to be constantly watched, so you can chop the vegetables or fix the rest of your meal while it cooks.

Makes 3 to 4 cups of barley, plus vegetables.

1 medium onion
3 garlic cloves
Extra virgin olive oil

1 cup barley

4 cups chicken or vegetable broth, divided

2 to 4 cups mixed, chopped vegetables,
  such as:
  ⊚ Asparagus
  ⊚ Broccoli
  ⊚ Bell peppers
  ⊚ Green beans
  ⊚ Spinach
  ⊚ Mushrooms
¼ to ½ teaspoon salt
Several generous grindings of pepper

1. Chop the onion and garlic. Coat the bottom of a stockpot with olive oil (about 2 tablespoons), and sauté the onion and garlic over medium-high heat.

2. When the onion and garlic are soft, add the barley and stir to coat.

3. Add 2 cups broth to the barley mixture. To keep it from sticking, stir occasionally.

4. While the barley is cooking, chop the vegetables.

5. When the broth is almost absorbed, add 1 cup broth, stirring occasionally.

6. When the broth is almost absorbed, turn the heat to low, add the remaining 1 cup broth, and stir occasionally.

7. When the final cup of broth is almost absorbed (after a total of about 50 minutes), add the crispy vegetables (such as asparagus, broccoli, peppers or green beans) and continue cooking another 5 minutes. If you're using soft vegetables (such as spinach or mushrooms), stir those in at the very end. Add salt and pepper to taste before serving.

 Variations

⊚ Stir in ½ to 1 cup Parmesan cheese before serving.

⊚ For softer vegetables, sauté the crispy vegetables during step 1 or add them when you add the last cup of broth in step 6.

⊚ Sauté a peeled, cubed delicata squash or sweet potato with the onions and garlic in step 1.

⊚ Add a can of white beans (rinsed and drained) in step 6 or 7.

⊚ Use short-grain brown rice instead of barley.

 Love Thy Leftovers

Toss in cubed *Basic Cooked Chicken* (page 74) or *Turkey Sausage* (page 86).

Barley Veggie Salad

Makes about 7 cups.

BARLEY

3 cups chicken or vegetable broth

1 cup barley

DRESSING

1 garlic clove

2 to 4 sprigs of cilantro

Juice of 1 lime (about 2 tablespoons)

1 tablespoon white wine vinegar

4 tablespoons extra virgin olive oil

Dash of honey

¼ to ½ teaspoon ground cumin

¼ teaspoon salt

Several generous grindings of pepper

3 to 4 cups mixed, chopped vegetables, such as:

- Unpeeled carrots
- Onions
- Zucchini
- Red or green bell peppers
- Grape or cherry tomatoes
- Baby spinach

1. In a medium saucepan, bring the broth to a boil over medium-high heat. Once the broth is boiling, add the barley.

2. Reduce the heat to low, cover the pan with a tightly fitting lid, and simmer for 50 minutes.

3. Turn off the flame and let the barley sit for about 10 minutes, without removing the cover. If there is still liquid in the pot, stir and let sit, uncovered, for an additional 10 minutes.

4. While the barley is cooking:

   a. Finely mince the garlic and cilantro. Combine with the remaining dressing ingredients in a small glass jar and shake well, or whisk together in a small bowl.

   b. Dice the carrots, onions, zucchini and peppers; halve the tomatoes; and shred the spinach into thin strips.

5. When the barley is done, transfer it to a large bowl, add the dressing, and toss lightly. Add the vegetables and toss again. Add additional salt and pepper to taste before serving. Serve at room temperature.

Divine Design: Barley

Intelligently designed with nearly every nutrient (in ideal proportions), barley fights heart disease by lowering cholesterol levels. It also improves digestion and helps prevent cancer. Maybe this is why the Bible mentions barley thirty-seven times—more than any other grain.

Variations

- Experiment by using different whole grains (such as rice) instead of the barley.
- Use bottled dressing instead of making your own.

Mix and Match Whole Grain Pasta

The options for pasta-based meals are endless. Just match the cooked whole grain pasta of your choice with a vegetable, a sauce and a protein.

Makes 2 to 3 servings.

PASTA

Many grocery stores carry whole grain pasta—rotini, linguini and penne are most common. Just remember: "Wheat pasta" is not the same as "whole wheat pasta," and "rice pasta" is not the same as "brown rice pasta." Of course, using spaghetti squash instead of traditional pasta is a great way to sneak more vegetables into your meal.

VEGETABLES

Unless you are using leftover *Basic Roasted Vegetables* (page 15), start by chopping your vegetables and sautéing them in olive oil. Onions and garlic are delicious staples that you can combine with any others on this list.

SAUCE

The amount of sauce to use will vary, depending on your personal preference. If you do not have the time or ingredients to prepare pasta sauce, just sauté garlic in extra virgin olive oil and lemon juice. Then sauté the other vegetables and stir in your protein. Add just enough additional oil and lemon juice to coat.

PROTEIN

If your protein is raw meat, the first step should be cooking it. Then add your vegetables and a little more oil. If your meat is already cooked, add it after you sauté your vegetables. If you are using cheese or pine nuts, sprinkle on top of your finished dish.

PASTA (8 ounces)	VEGETABLES (2 to 4 cups)	SAUCE	PROTEIN
Brown rice pasta	Asparagus	*Balsamic Vinaigrette* (page 23) or store-bought Italian dressing (toss with cold pasta and vegetables to create pasta salad)	*Old-Fashioned Meat Sauce* (page 90, no additional sauce needed)
Corn pasta	*Basic Roasted Vegetables* (page 15)	Extra virgin olive oil, lemon juice and garlic	1 to 2 cups cubed *Basic Cooked Chicken* (page 74)
Quinoa pasta	Green beans	Extra virgin olive oil and fresh herbs (such as basil, rosemary and/or oregano)	1 can of tuna, drained and flaked
Spaghetti Squash (page 20)	Leeks	*Marinara Sauce* (page 32)	1 to 2 cups lean ground beef, turkey or chicken
Whole spelt pasta	Primavera (zucchini, yellow squash, spinach, red/yellow/green peppers, onions, garlic, tomatoes, carrots, eggplant, mushrooms)	*Pesto* (page 33)	1 to 2 cups *Turkey Sausage* (page 86)
Whole wheat pasta	Swiss chard or kale	Store-bought pasta sauce	1 cup cheese (feta, Parmesan, goat, mozzarella)
	Sun-dried tomatoes, rehydrated		½ cup pine nuts
			1 cup white beans
			1 to 2 cups *Basic Cooked Fish* (page 63)

Asian Quinoa Salad

Makes about 4 cups.

1 cup quinoa
2 cups chicken or vegetable broth

1-inch piece of fresh ginger
3 green onions (white and some green)
¼ bunch cilantro (mostly leaves)
1 garlic clove

2 tablespoons extra virgin olive oil
1 tablespoon honey
Juice of ¾ lemon (about 3 tablespoons)
1 teaspoon salt
Several generous grindings of pepper

½ cup peanuts

1. If you are not using prewashed quinoa, wash the quinoa well using a fine mesh strainer. (If the quinoa can fit through your strainer's holes, line it with a coffee filter first.)

2. Combine the quinoa and broth in a medium saucepan. Bring the broth to a boil, reduce the heat, and simmer until the liquid is absorbed, about 20 minutes. (The quinoa is done when the grain becomes transparent and the spiral-like germ separates.)

3. While the quinoa is cooking:

   a. Peel and grate the ginger and add to a medium bowl.

   b. Chop the green onions and cilantro and add to the bowl.

   c. Finely chop the garlic and add to the bowl.

   d. Add the remaining ingredients (except the peanuts) to the bowl and mix to incorporate.

   e. Chop the peanuts and set aside.

4. Cool the cooked quinoa slightly, add to the mixture in the bowl, and mix thoroughly.

5. Sprinkle the peanuts over the salad before serving. Add additional salt and pepper to taste. Serve warm, at room temperature or cold.

 Divine Design: Quinoa

Iron deficiency in your diet can cause a lack of oxygen in your blood cells, which can make you feel fatigued. Including quinoa in your diet provides you with lots of God-given nutrients, including a generous helping of iron to boost your energy.

Variation

To serve as an entrée, for each portion, spread 1 tablespoon peanut butter over a large lettuce leaf or a whole wheat tortilla. Top with ⅓ cup quinoa salad, roll up, and serve.

Millet Casserole

We usually add a protein such as chicken or beans to Millet Casserole so that we end up with a main dish (see the variations). To save time, prepare extra millet a day or two ahead and then use 3 cups for this recipe and 1 cup for breakfast.

Makes 5 to 6 cups.

¾ cup millet
2¼ cups water
(or 3 cups cooked millet)

1 medium onion
2 garlic cloves

2 to 3 cups mixed, chopped vegetables, such as:
- Unpeeled carrots
- Zucchini
- Red or green bell peppers
- Grape or cherry tomatoes
- Baby spinach

1 teaspoon dried basil
1 teaspoon dried oregano
¼ teaspoon salt
3 cups *Marinara Sauce* (page 32)
(or 1, 25-ounce jar of pasta sauce)

½ cup Parmesan cheese, divided

1. Cook the millet in the water according to package instructions or the directions in *Hot Millet Cereal* (page 150), omitting the salt.

2. Preheat the oven to 375 degrees.

3. Chop the onion and mince the garlic.

4. Chop the vegetables.

5. In a large bowl combine the millet, onion, garlic and vegetables with the remaining ingredients (except for ¼ cup Parmesan cheese).

6. Transfer the millet mixture to an 8 x 8-inch baking pan, and sprinkle the remaining cheese on top of the casserole.

7. Bake, uncovered, for 35 minutes, or until the top begins to turn golden brown.

 Variations

- For a main dish, add 2 to 3 cups diced *Basic Cooked Chicken* (page 74) or 1 to 2 cups *Turkey Sausage* (page 86) in step 5.

- For a meatless main, add 1, 15-ounce can of white beans (rinsed and drained) in step 5.

 Love Thy Leftovers

For a millet and vegetable stir-fry, in a large frying pan sauté chopped asparagus, broccoli, spinach or other vegetables in olive oil until they begin to soften. Add the leftover Millet Casserole. Stir to combine and cook until heated through. If desired, sprinkle with additional Parmesan cheese.

Millet Pilaf

Makes about 4 cups.

½ cup millet
1½ cups water
(Or 2 cups cooked millet)

_____

1 medium onion
2 garlic cloves
1 unpeeled carrot
½ to ⅔ cup pecans
½ to ⅔ cup dried fruit (dark raisins, golden raisins, diced dried apricots or a combination)
2 tablespoons extra virgin olive oil

_____

½ cup frozen peas
½ teaspoon cinnamon
Several dashes of ground nutmeg
Several dashes of ground cumin
¼ to ½ teaspoon salt
Several generous grindings of pepper

1. Cook the millet in the water according to package instructions or the directions in _Hot Millet Cereal_ (page 150), omitting the salt.

2. While the millet cooks:

   a. Chop the onion, garlic, carrot, pecans and apricots (if using).

   b. Sauté the onion and garlic in the olive oil in a large frying pan over medium-high heat.

   c. Once the onion and garlic begin to soften, add the carrots and cook until they just begin to soften.

3. Add the millet, pecans, dried fruit and remaining ingredients to the pan and stir to combine. Add additional seasoning if needed. Heat through and serve hot or at room temperature.

 Divine Design: Millet

God loves you so much that He designed millet—low in fat, and high in vitamins, minerals and protein—to nourish you.

Variation

Use cooked quinoa in place of the millet.

Polenta with Spinach and Feta

The texture of this recipe will be soft and creamy. Serve as a grain side dish or as a stand-alone meal.

Makes 4 servings.

5 cups chicken or vegetable broth
1 tablespoon extra virgin olive oil

1 cup polenta or coarsely ground cornmeal

2 cups firmly packed fresh spinach
¼ to ½ cup chopped tomatoes (optional)
¼ to ½ cup finely chopped onions (optional)
¼ to ½ cup chopped red bell pepper (optional)

4 to 6 ounces crumbled feta cheese, or more to taste
Salt and pepper to taste
¼ cup pine nuts or chopped walnuts (optional)

1. In a medium saucepan, bring the broth and olive oil to a boil over medium-high heat.

2. Add the polenta to the saucepan and whisk together the polenta and broth, removing any lumps.

3. Reduce the heat to a simmer and allow the polenta to cook for about 25 to 30 minutes, uncovered. To keep it from sticking, stir every 4 or 5 minutes. During this time, the polenta will thicken.

4. While the polenta is cooking, chop the spinach and any other vegetables that you are using (tomatoes, onions or pepper).

5. When the polenta is cooked, remove from the heat and add the chopped vegetables, feta, salt, pepper and pine nuts (if using). Mix to incorporate.

Divine Design: Corn

What is polenta? It's simply a mush made from coarsely ground corn, which God made high in carbohydrates, fiber, vitamins and minerals, and low in fat. While corn is technically a vegetable, its high starch content causes many to classify it as a grain.

Variations

⊙ Substitute 4 ounces goat cheese and 2 to 4 tablespoons chopped fresh sage (2 teaspoons dry) for the feta cheese.

⊙ Sauté the onion and any crispy vegetables in the olive oil during step 1. Then add the broth and bring to a boil.

⊙ Add *Turkey Sausage* (page 86) during the last 10 minutes of cooking.

⊙ For a firmer polenta that can be used as a bed for chicken or fish, simply reduce the amount of broth to 3 or 4 cups.

Love Thy Leftovers

Reheat leftover polenta in a frying pan with olive oil and additional vegetables, or reheat it, uncovered, in a 350 degree oven for about 15 minutes, or until the top begins to brown.

Polenta Pizza

Makes 4 servings.

CRUST

2 cups chicken or vegetable broth

½ cup milk or rice milk

¼ teaspoon salt

¾ cup polenta or coarsely ground cornmeal

¼ cup Parmesan cheese

VEGETABLE OPTIONS (USE ANY COMBINATION TO YIELD 1 TO 2 CUPS)

- Tomatoes
- Spinach
- Asparagus
- Broccoli
- Onions
- Green, red or yellow bell peppers

SAUCE OPTIONS

- *Marinara Sauce* (page 32) or store-bought pasta sauce
- *Pesto* (page 33)
- *Roasted Garlic Spread* (page 193)
- Store-bought pizza sauce
- Extra virgin olive oil

CHEESE OPTIONS

- Feta cheese, crumbled
- Goat cheese, crumbled
- Parmesan cheese, grated or shredded
- Mozzarella cheese, shredded

1. Preheat the oven to 350 degrees and oil an 8 x 8-inch baking pan.

2. In a medium saucepan bring the broth, milk and salt to a boil over medium-high heat. Slowly add the polenta and whisk until the liquid is absorbed, about 10 minutes. Stir in ¼ cup Parmesan cheese.

3. Scrape the polenta into the prepared pan. While the polenta sets, finely dice the vegetables of your choice.

4. When the polenta crust is firm (about 10 minutes), top with a thin layer of your choice of sauce. Top with your choice of cheese and the chopped vegetables.

5. Bake for 12 to 18 minutes, or until the cheese is bubbly and the vegetables are cooked.

6. Slice the pizza into squares and serve.

Divine Design: Corn

God filled corn with insoluble fiber—the type that protects against heart disease, eases constipation and reduces the risk of colon cancer.

 Variations

- Add pine nuts, chopped walnuts or cubed *Basic Cooked Chicken* (page 74) to the pizza.

- Rehydrate (by soaking in hot water) and dice a few sun-dried tomatoes. Sprinkle these on top of the pizza.

Basic Roasted Potatoes

Makes 3 servings.

1 pound unpeeled potatoes (any variety, including sweet potatoes)

---

1 tablespoon extra virgin olive oil

Several dashes of salt

Several generous grindings of pepper

OPTIONAL SEASONINGS (USE ABOUT 1 TEASPOON)

- Cajun Spice Mix from *Cajun-Spiced Pumpkin Seeds* (page 200)
- Ground cumin and chili powder
- Dried rosemary and/or oregano
- Commercial seasoning mix (such as Italian seasoning)

1. Preheat the oven to 400 degrees.

2. Cut the potatoes into uniform pieces so they cook evenly: Simply keep cutting them in half until you get your desired size. Or slice them in half (the long way) and then into wedges, so they look like steak fries.

3. Put the potatoes, olive oil, salt, pepper and any seasonings in a large bowl and toss to completely coat. Transfer the potatoes to a shallow roasting pan or a jelly roll pan.

4. Bake for 20 minutes, stir with a rubber spatula or wooden spoon, and return to the oven.

5. Check the potatoes every 10 minutes or so. Cook for 30 to 45 minutes, depending on the size and type of the potatoes. They are done when they turn golden brown and are easily pierced with a fork.

 Divine Design: Potatoes

Keep their covering on! In their original God-given form, potatoes are filled with fiber—but once you remove the skin, little fiber remains.

 Variations

- When you toss the potatoes in step 3, add a thickly sliced onion and/or minced garlic and add a little extra oil.

- Bake the potatoes without the optional seasonings. After removing them from the oven, toss lightly with balsamic vinegar, additional olive oil, Dijon mustard, lemon juice and minced fresh rosemary.

Love Thy Leftovers

- Toss leftover roasted potatoes with *Green Bean and Tomato Salad with Garlic Basil Dressing* (page 8) and a can of tuna (drained and flaked).

- For breakfast, serve reheated diced roasted potatoes with *Basic Scrambled Eggs* (page 152).

- Add leftover roasted potatoes to *"Cream" of Potato Soup* (page 131), *Vegetable Chili* (page 135) or *Meat Chili* (page 133).

Classic Potato Salad

If you want to cut the potatoes ahead of time but don't want them to turn brown, simply soak them in water until you are ready to use them.

Makes 4 to 5 servings.

POTATOES

1½ pounds unpeeled potatoes (any variety)

1 to 2 unpeeled carrots

½ medium onion (red or yellow) or 2 green onions (white and some green)

OPTIONAL INGREDIENTS (ADD UP TO 1 CUP)

- 1 to 2 celery stalks, diced
- 1 to 2 hard-boiled eggs, diced (see *Egg Salad,* page 112, for cooking method)
- ½ to 1 cup firmly packed spinach, shredded

DRESSING

¼ cup plain yogurt

¼ cup mayonnaise

1 tablespoon Dijon mustard

¼ teaspoon dried marjoram or oregano

¼ to ½ teaspoon salt

Several generous grindings of pepper

1. Cut the potatoes into ½-inch cubes, place in a stockpot, and add just enough water to cover the potatoes.

2. Bring the water to a boil over high heat and cook the potatoes until tender, about 15 to 20 minutes. While the potatoes cook:

   a. Dice the carrots. Add to a large bowl.

   b. Finely dice the onion and add to the bowl, along with any optional ingredients.

   c. Prepare the dressing by adding the dressing ingredients to a small bowl and mixing well to incorporate.

3. When the potatoes are tender, remove from the heat and drain well.

4. Allow the potatoes to cool slightly for 5 to 10 minutes, and add them to the bowl of vegetables, along with the dressing. Mix well to incorporate and chill before serving. Add additional salt or other seasonings to taste before serving.

 Variations

- Add 1 to 2 tablespoons capers and/or some finely chopped parsley to the potato salad.
- Experiment with different proportions of mayonnaise and yogurt.

 Love Thy Leftovers

Add a can of tuna (drained and flaked) or cubed *Basic Cooked Chicken* (page 74) to leftover potato salad.

Potato Pancakes

If your salad spinner's holes are smaller than the size of your potato shreds, spinning is a great way to drain the liquid. Serve the potato pancakes with *Applesauce* (page 181).

Makes about 12, 3-inch pancakes.

1 unpeeled medium potato (any variety)

1 unpeeled medium sweet potato

1 medium onion

Juice of ½ lemon (about 2 tablespoons)

½ teaspoon salt

2 eggs

⅓ cup flour (whole wheat, whole spelt, oat or a combination)

Several generous grindings of pepper

Extra virgin olive oil for frying

1. Preheat the oven to 200 degrees.

2. Using a food processor or hand grater, shred the potatoes and onion.

3. Spoon the shredded potatoes and onion into a salad spinner. Spin out the liquid and add the potatoes and onion to a large bowl. (Or transfer the potatoes and onion to a colander and press out the liquid.)

4. Add the next five ingredients (lemon juice through pepper) to the bowl. Mix well to incorporate. If the potato mixture looks soupy, add another tablespoon or two of flour.

5. Pour enough olive oil into a frying pan to lightly coat the bottom of the pan, and heat to medium-high.

6. Scoop up the mixture using a heaping ¼-cup measure and drop onto the pan. Cook until golden brown and crispy on both sides, about 5 to 7 minutes per side.

7. Keep the potato pancakes on a cookie sheet in a 200 degree oven until you are ready to serve them.

 Divine Design: Sweet Potatoes

Sweet potatoes are fat-free, low-calorie disease fighters. The risk of heart disease, cancer and stroke can be lowered by eating this intelligently designed superstar spud.

 Variations

⊙ Substitute a medium zucchini or yellow squash for one of the potatoes.

⊙ Add a carrot in step 2.

⊙ Add a few ounces of feta cheese in step 4.

♥ Love Thy Leftovers

⊙ Potato pancakes keep in the refrigerator for several days. Reheat in a 350 degree oven or toaster oven for 10 minutes.

⊙ Eat leftover potato pancakes as a snack, or serve them with *Basic Scrambled Eggs* (page 152) for breakfast.

Mashed Potatoes with a Twist

Makes 3 servings.

1 unpeeled medium potato (any variety)
1 unpeeled medium sweet potato
2 garlic cloves

Extra virgin olive oil
¼ to 1 cup milk or rice milk

¼ teaspoon salt
Several generous grindings of pepper

1. Cut the potatoes into 1-inch chunks and cut the garlic cloves in half.

2. Put the potatoes and garlic in a medium saucepan and cover them with water.

3. Bring the water to a boil and cook the potatoes until they are tender and can be easily pierced with a fork, about 15 to 20 minutes.

4. Drain the potatoes and garlic in a colander.

5. Return the potatoes and garlic to the pot. Add a few splashes of olive oil to the potatoes and mash using a potato masher, hand mixer or wooden spoon.

6. Continue mashing the potatoes and add milk, a few tablespoons at a time, until they reach the desired consistency. For smoother potatoes, add them to a food processor and puree.

7. Add salt and pepper to taste.

 Variations

- Use broth instead of milk.

- Add chopped fresh herbs, such as parsley, rosemary or basil in step 6.

- Sauté chopped onions or leeks in olive oil and add to the potatoes in step 5.

- Add a peeled and chopped large celery root and the chopped white part of two large leeks to the pot during step 2 and increase the water. When the vegetables are soft, drain and transfer to a food processor. Process until smooth, adding milk as necessary and salt and pepper to taste.

 Love Thy Leftovers

- Sauté leftover mashed potatoes with olive oil and fresh spinach, or with leftover *Basic Roasted Vegetables* (page 15).

- Stir in cubed *Basic Cooked Chicken* (page 74), or top with feta cheese.

- Use leftover potatoes to make *"Cream" of Potato Soup* (page 131).

Potato Salad with Green Beans

Makes 6 servings.

2 pounds unpeeled potatoes (any variety)
2 tablespoons extra virgin olive oil
Several dashes of salt
Several generous grindings of pepper

½ pound green beans
1 small red onion
½ pint grape or cherry tomatoes

BASIL VINAIGRETTE
1 garlic clove
6 tablespoons extra virgin olive oil
2 tablespoons white wine vinegar
20 to 30 fresh basil leaves (about ¼ cup firmly packed)
¼ to ½ teaspoon salt
Several generous grindings of pepper

1. Preheat the oven to 400 degrees.

2. Cut the potatoes into ½-inch cubes and put the potatoes, olive oil, salt and pepper into a large bowl. Toss to completely coat and transfer the potatoes to a shallow roasting pan or a jelly roll pan.

3. Bake the potatoes for 20 minutes, stir with a rubber spatula or wooden spoon, and return to the oven. Then begin checking them every 10 minutes or so. Depending on the size and type of your potatoes, the total cooking time will range from 30 to 45 minutes. They are done when they turn golden brown and are tender when pierced with a fork.

4. While the potatoes cook:

   a. Break off the stem ends from the green beans and add to the potatoes during the last 5 to 7 minutes of baking.

   b. Dice the onion and add to a large bowl; add the tomatoes to the bowl.

   c. Prepare the dressing: chop the garlic in a food processor, add the remaining dressing ingredients, and process until smooth.

5. After the potatoes and green beans have cooked and cooled, add them to the bowl with the onions and tomatoes. Add the dressing and toss. Serve at room temperature.

Divine Design: Green Beans

Green beans are an excellent source of vitamin K. God designed this important vitamin to give you strong bones. Vitamin K also helps stop the bleeding after you cut yourself, since it aids blood coagulation and clotting.

 Love Thy Leftovers

- Toss in a can of tuna (drained and flaked) with leftover potato salad; serve on a bed of greens.

- Add extra tomatoes, onions, diced carrots or other vegetables to leftover potato salad. If the salad needs more dressing, add a dash of olive oil and white wine vinegar.

Chapter 3
Fish, Poultry, Beef and Lamb

FISH

Basic Cooked Fish

Tuna Salad

Pesto-Crusted Salmon

Salmon with Horseradish Crust

Maple Almond Salmon

Salmon with Leeks

Apricot-Glazed Tuna

Halibut with Salsa

Halibut with Peppers and Capers

Mustard Dill Sole

Pecan-Crusted Tilapia

POULTRY

Basic Cooked Chicken

Chicken Salad with Pecans and Grapes

Chicken with Peanut Sauce

Mustard Herb Chicken

Asian Chicken

Chicken with Peanut and Coconut
  Crust

Roasted Chicken

Sweet Balsamic Chicken

Tandoori Chicken

Turkey Pot Pie

Turkey Sausage

BEEF AND LAMB

Beef Brisket

Gyros

Meat Loaf

Old-Fashioned Meat Sauce

Tamale Pie

Vietnamese Beef Salad

SEE ALSO . . .

In the Bible, God makes it clear to Noah that eating animals is permissible (Genesis 9:3).

A millennia or so later, God spells out which animals He designed to be eaten and which He did not. What's on God's menu? Here is a brief overview of these guidelines, adapted from *Holy Cow! Does God Care about What We Eat?* (First Fruits of Zion, 2005).

Mammals (Leviticus 11:3–8): God gives two parameters for eating mammals. To qualify for food, they must have a "split hoof" and must "chew the cud." *Split hooves* means that the animal's feet are entirely wrapped with a hard covering that is fully split from front to back. *Chewing the cud* is a complex digestion process. Animals that chew their cud (known as *ruminants*) have several stomachs that food passes through before being excreted. Animals that qualify as ruminants include cows, sheep and goats. Pigs do not qualify because they do not chew their cud.

Fish (Leviticus 11:9–12): According to Leviticus 11:9, edible fish must have fins and scales. Heart-healthy favorites such as salmon, halibut, tuna, mahi-mahi, flounder, sole, anchovies, cod, bass, grouper, haddock, perch, snapper, sardines and trout all qualify. Scavengers such as shellfish (shrimp, lobster, oysters and clams), catfish and shark are excluded.

Birds (Leviticus 11:13–19): God does not give distinguishing characteristics for clean birds. Rather, the Bible lists examples of unclean birds. As with fish, unclean birds (such as vultures and buzzards) are generally scavengers that God designed for purposes other than to be eaten. Commonly eaten poultry, such as chicken, turkey and duck, are considered clean.

A thorough list of clean and unclean animals appears in Appendix B.

The Bible also forbids eating blood. This frequent command, along with God's comments about how an animal is to be killed, is the driving force behind the tradition of eating *kosher* meat. This topic, plus the topics of organic meat and the tradition of separating meat and milk are addressed further in *Holy Cow!*

While God allows people to eat certain types of meat, the optimal amount is unclear. Your body (and the planet) is designed for you to eat much less of these creatures than most folks do. In fact, the USDA's recommended serving size of beef or chicken is about the size of a deck of cards. That's certainly food for thought as you decide how much meat is right for you.

Principle 1

Thankfully, God clearly explains which animals He designed for food and which He did not. See Appendix B for the list, which is based on God's descriptions in Leviticus 11.

Principle 2

Animals that eat only the vegetable-based foods described in Genesis 1:29 are closer to God's design than those that do not. Ideally, cows are designed to eat only grass. Your body will stay healthier if you avoid eating meat that comes from animals that have been exposed to antibiotics, growth hormones and other man-made substances.

Principle 3

Instead of sharing the cultural obsession with the frequent intake of large meat portions, consider eating higher-quality meat in smaller amounts and less often.

Basic Cooked Fish

Makes 4 servings.

1 pound skinless fish fillets (salmon, tilapia or any other flaky fish)

Extra virgin olive oil

Several dashes of salt

Several generous grindings of pepper

OPTIONAL TOPPINGS

- ⊚ Several sprigs of fresh thyme per fillet, whole or chopped
- ⊚ 1 sprig of fresh rosemary per fillet, whole or chopped
- ⊚ 1 garlic clove per fillet, chopped
- ⊚ 1 medium onion, thinly sliced or chopped

1 lemon or lime

1. Preheat the oven to 400 degrees.

2. Wash the fish, pat dry with a paper towel, and place in an 8 x 8-inch baking pan.

3. Brush the fish with olive oil and lightly sprinkle it with salt and pepper.

4. Sprinkle the fish with the fresh herbs or chopped garlic (if using). Arrange the onion slices (if using) over the fish pieces.

5. Thinly slice the lemon or lime and arrange the slices over the fish pieces.

6. Bake the fish for about 10 minutes per inch of thickness, or until it flakes easily with a fork.

 Variation

Prepare the fish as directed above, but instead of baking it, place the fish in a steamer and cook using the same time guidelines.

Tuna Salad

Makes about 3 cups.

1 unpeeled carrot

1 small onion

2, 6-ounce cans of tuna packed in water

2 tablespoons mayonnaise

2 tablespoons plain yogurt

Several dashes of salt

Several generous grindings of pepper

OPTIONAL INGREDIENTS
- Finely diced celery
- Finely diced green pepper
- Chopped kalamata olives
- Chopped artichoke hearts
- Chopped fresh parsley, dill or cilantro
- Dijon mustard
- Prepared horseradish
- Pickle relish (or finely diced pickles)
- Lemon juice

1. Finely chop the carrot and onion.

2. Drain the tuna and flake it into tiny pieces.

3. In a large bowl combine the carrot, onion, tuna and the remaining ingredients, including any optional ingredients. Mix thoroughly and adjust seasonings to taste.

4. Serve immediately or chill until ready to use.

Divine Design: Onions

The intelligent design of onions includes sulfur compounds that prevent and reduce inflammation. This wonderful veggie helps stop asthma and even treats inflammation caused by insect bites.

 ## Variations

- For a more finely chopped tuna salad, combine the ingredients and any optional ingredients you are using in a food processor and process until you reach the desired consistency.

- Experiment with different proportions of mayonnaise and yogurt, or use equal parts mayonnaise, yogurt and olive oil.

- Use canned salmon instead of tuna. Look for brands that use wild Alaskan salmon without skin or bones.

Pesto-Crusted Salmon

Makes 4 servings.

1 bunch parsley (mostly leaves)

2 tablespoons fresh thyme

2 tablespoons fresh rosemary

1 tablespoon fresh oregano

2 to 3 green onions (white and some green)
  or ¼ medium onion

⅓ cup pine nuts or walnuts

Heaping ½ teaspoon salt

Several generous grindings of pepper

⅓ cup extra virgin olive oil

1 pound skinless salmon fillets

1. Preheat the oven to 400 degrees.

2. Prepare the pesto:

   a. Combine the first eight ingredients (parsley through pepper) in a food processor and process until the mixture is well chopped.

   b. While the food processor is running, slowly pour the olive oil through the feed tube. Process until smooth.

3. Wash the salmon fillets, pat dry, and place in an 8 x 8-inch baking pan.

4. Spread a ¼-inch layer of pesto evenly over the top and sides of the salmon.

5. Bake until the salmon flakes easily with a fork and begins to turn opaque, about 12 to 15 minutes, depending on the thickness of the salmon.

Divine Design: Salmon

Fish oil, one of God's greatest creations, helps people of all shapes and sizes. Especially notable are the benefits for women: fish oil reduces menstrual cramping and fights prostaglandins, which cause heart problems and promote cancerous growths that lead to breast cancer.

Variations

⊙ Use either version of *Pesto* (page 33) instead of the pesto indicated here.

⊙ Use any flaky white fish such as tilapia or cod.

⊙ Spread the pesto over boneless, skinless chicken breasts and cook according to the directions for *Basic Cooked Chicken* (page 74), omitting the other ingredients.

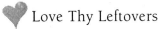

Love Thy Leftovers

⊙ Use extra pesto to top baked potatoes, *Basic Cooked Rice* (page 39) or *Basic Roasted Vegetables* (page 15).

⊙ Stir leftover pesto into *Spinach and Cilantro Green Rice* (page 43).

Salmon with Horseradish Crust

Makes 4 servings.

⅓ cup almonds

⅓ cup prepared horseradish

1 pound skinless salmon fillets

1. Preheat the oven to 400 degrees.

2. Finely grind the almonds in a food processor or blender.

3. Combine the horseradish and almond meal in a small bowl.

4. Wash and pat dry the salmon and place in an 8 x 8-inch baking pan.

5. Thinly spread the horseradish mixture evenly over the top and the sides of the salmon. (There might be some leftover mixture.)

6. Bake until the salmon flakes easily with a fork and begins to turn opaque, about 12 to 15 minutes, depending on the thickness of the salmon.

 Divine Design: Horseradish

A great addition to a meaty meal, this God-given bitter herb kick-starts the digestion process and helps your body break down fats.

 Variation

Use 3 tablespoons Dijon or stone-ground mustard instead of the horseradish.

Maple Almond Salmon

Makes 4 servings.

2 tablespoons almonds

2 tablespoons Dijon mustard

2 tablespoons maple syrup

2 teaspoons balsamic vinegar

Scant ¼ teaspoon salt

Several generous grindings of pepper

1 pound skinless salmon fillets

1. Coarsely chop the almonds and combine with the next five ingredients (mustard through pepper) in a plastic zipper bag.

2. Wash the fish, pat dry with a paper towel, and cut into 2-inch wide pieces. Add the fish pieces to the plastic zipper bag.

3. Refrigerate and allow the fish to marinate for 30 minutes.

4. When you are ready to cook the fish, preheat the oven to 400 degrees.

5. Pour the fish and marinade into an 8 x 8-inch baking pan, and bake until the salmon flakes easily with a fork and begins to turn opaque, about 10 to 12 minutes, depending on the thickness of the salmon.

Divine Design: Salmon

Arthritis sufferers can find relief in the Creator's design for fish. The omega-3 fatty acids found in them ease painful inflammation of the joints, providing relief the natural way.

Variations

⊚ Skip the marinating step. Instead, spread the maple almond mixture over the fish until each piece is evenly coated and bake immediately.

⊚ Use any flaky white fish, such as tilapia or cod.

⊚ For honey mustard fish, omit the almonds and substitute honey for the maple syrup, or simply use ⅓ cup *Honey Mustard Dressing* (page 30).

Salmon with Leeks

Leeks are like giant green onions. Since dirt is often trapped between the layers, make sure to clean the leeks well before using.

Makes 4 servings.

2 medium leeks

Extra virgin olive oil

Several dashes of salt
Several generous grindings of pepper

1 pound skinless salmon fillets

1. Preheat the oven to 400 degrees.

2. Wash the leeks very well. Cut the leeks to use all of the white and 1 inch of the light green (discard the rest) and thinly slice.

3. Coat the bottom of a frying pan with olive oil (about 2 tablespoons), and sauté the leeks over medium-high heat.

4. Sauté the leeks until they are soft and begin to "sweat," about 10 minutes. Add several dashes of salt and several generous grindings of pepper, and mix to incorporate.

5. While the leeks are cooking, wash the salmon and pat dry.

6. When the leeks are cooked, transfer them to an 8 x 8-inch baking pan.

7. Brush the salmon with olive oil and lightly salt and pepper both sides. Place the salmon fillets on top of the leeks.

8. Bake until the salmon flakes easily with a fork and begins to turn opaque, about 12 to 15 minutes, depending on the thickness of the salmon. The leeks will also begin to brown.

Divine Design: Leeks

Leeks, part of the onion family, were given by God not only to flavor your food but also to treat kidney problems, promote weight loss and treat coughs.

Apricot-Glazed Tuna

Makes 4 servings.

1-inch piece of fresh ginger

2 garlic cloves
⅛ medium red onion

2 teaspoons sesame oil or extra virgin olive oil

1½ tablespoons soy sauce or tamari
½ cup apricot all-fruit spread

1 pound tuna steaks

1. Preheat the oven to 400 degrees.

2. Peel the ginger and grate or finely chop it.

3. Chop the garlic and onion.

4. Add the oil to a small saucepan and sauté the ginger, garlic and onion over medium heat for 1 to 2 minutes.

5. Add the soy sauce and all-fruit spread to the saucepan, reduce the heat to low, and bring the glaze to a slow boil. Simmer for 2 minutes.

6. While the glaze heats, wash the tuna, pat dry with a paper towel, and place in an 8 x 8-inch baking pan.

7. Pour the glaze over the tuna steaks, reserving about ¼ cup as a dipping sauce for the cooked tuna.

8. Bake for 10 to 15 minutes, until the tuna is at the desired doneness. If cooking longer than 15 minutes, place foil over the fish to prevent the glaze from burning.

9. Serve with any additional glaze.

 Variations

- Use salmon or any other fish steak or fillet instead of the tuna.

- Marinate the fish in the glaze for 1 hour or more before baking.

- Substitute balsamic vinegar for the soy sauce.

- Use the *Asian Chicken* marinade (page 78) instead of the one indicated here.

Love Thy Leftovers

Add leftover baked tuna to a *Mix and Match Salad* (page 10).

Halibut with Salsa

The key to delicious Halibut with Salsa is buying high-quality salsa.

Makes 4 servings.

½ medium onion
2 cups mixed, chopped vegetables, such as:
  ◉ Red or yellow bell peppers
  ◉ Unpeeled carrots
  ◉ Zucchini
Extra virgin olive oil

———————————

Juice of 1 lime (about 2 tablespoons)
1 cup salsa

———————————

1 pound skinless halibut fillets
Several dashes of salt
Several generous grindings of pepper

1. Chop the onion and vegetables.

2. Coat the bottom of a frying pan with olive oil (about 2 tablespoons) and sauté the onions and other vegetables over medium-high heat until the vegetables are soft, about 5 to 10 minutes.

3. Add the lime juice and salsa, stir, and reduce the heat to low.

4. Wash the fish, pat dry with a paper towel, and place in the frying pan.

5. Sprinkle the fish with salt and pepper, and spoon the sauce over the fish.

6. Cover the pan and simmer for 15 minutes, or until the fish flakes easily with a fork.

 Divine Design: Halibut

To help relieve pain, reduce inflammation and protect against heart disease, eat more fish. Fish were created by God to provide essential omega-3 fatty acids that can't be produced by your own body. Your body will thank you for making fish your main course.

Variations

Use Halibut with Salsa to make fish tacos. Simply break the cooked fish into pieces and put the fish and sauce mixture into a hard taco shell or whole grain tortilla. Add your favorite toppings, such as lettuce, cheese, chopped tomatoes, black olives or avocado.

Halibut with Peppers and Capers

Makes 4 servings.

1 medium onion

2 garlic cloves

1 red or yellow bell pepper

Extra virgin olive oil

2 medium tomatoes (or 1, 14-ounce can chopped tomatoes, drained)

¼ to ½ teaspoon salt

Several generous grindings of pepper

1 pound halibut fillets

Juice of ½ lemon or 1 lime (about 2 tablespoons)

Several dashes of salt

Several generous grindings of pepper

2 tablespoons capers

Up to ¼ cup broth or tomato juice (optional)

1. Preheat the oven to 400 degrees.

2. Chop the onion, garlic and pepper.

3. Coat the bottom of a frying pan with olive oil (about 2 tablespoons) and sauté the onion, garlic and pepper over medium-high heat until the vegetables are soft, about 5 to 10 minutes.

4. Chop the tomatoes and add to the pan, along with the salt and pepper. Stir, reduce the heat, and simmer until the onions are soft, about 10 minutes.

5. While the vegetables cook, prepare the halibut with olive oil, lemon juice, salt, and pepper, according to the directions for *Basic Cooked Fish* (page 63), omitting any optional toppings. (Pour the lemon juice over the fish instead of using lemon slices.)

6. While the fish bakes, stir the vegetable mixture, add the capers and broth, if using, and continue to simmer.

7. When the fish is done, serve on a platter with the vegetable mixture spooned over the top.

Divine Design: Bell Peppers

Eating bell peppers packs a double punch against cataracts. Sweet peppers, such as red and green bell peppers, are rich in vitamin C and beta-carotene—two essentials for taking care of your eyes.

Variations

- Instead of baking the halibut, poach it in the frying pan with the vegetable mixture (after step 3), as in the directions for *Halibut with Salsa* (page 70). Add additional broth or tomato juice if needed.

- Use 1 to 2 cups chopped vegetables, such as carrots and zucchini, instead of or in addition to the bell pepper.

- Substitute sliced or chopped olives for the capers.

Mustard Dill Sole

Makes 4 servings.

1 tablespoon extra virgin olive oil

2 tablespoons Dijon mustard

1 heaping teaspoon dried dill (or 3 to 4 sprigs of fresh dill, chopped)

Juice of ½ lemon (about 2 tablespoons)

Several generous grindings of pepper

1 pound sole or flounder fillets

1. Preheat the oven to 400 degrees.

2. Combine all of the ingredients (except the fish) in a small bowl.

3. Wash the fish, pat dry with a paper towel, and place on a jelly roll pan.

4. Spread the mustard mixture over the fish until it is evenly coated.

5. Bake for about 10 minutes, or until the fish flakes easily with a fork.

Divine Design: Sole

Sole fish varieties come from the flounder family. The Creator made flounder an excellent source of selenium to help protect against cancer, prevent asthma, fight depression and increase fertility in men.

Variation

⊕ Use cod fillets or any other fish fillet instead of sole, and place the fish in an 8 x 8-inch baking pan. You may need to increase the cooking time to 12 to 15 minutes.

⊕ Use any extra mustard mixture as a dipping sauce after the fish is cooked.

Pecan-Crusted Tilapia

Makes 4 servings.

⅓ cup corn flour or cornmeal

1½ teaspoons salt

Several generous grindings of pepper

Dash of cayenne pepper

1 egg white

2 tablespoons milk or rice milk

1 cup pecans

1 pound tilapia

1. Preheat the oven to 400 degrees and lightly oil an 8 x 8- or 9 x 13-inch baking pan.

2. Using 3 shallow bowls or 3 plates:

   a. Combine the cornmeal, salt, pepper and cayenne in the first bowl or plate.

   b. Beat the egg white and combine with the milk in the second bowl or plate.

   c. Finely chop the pecans and pour into the third bowl or plate.

3. Wash the tilapia and pat dry. Cut the fillets into pieces 2 inches wide.

4. For each piece of fish:

   a. Dredge in the cornmeal, lightly coating both sides.

   b. Dip in the egg mixture, wetting both sides.

   c. Dredge both sides in the pecans.

   d. Place the coated fish pieces in the prepared baking pan. Bake for 12 to 15 minutes, or until the fish flakes easily with a fork.

Divine Design: Tilapia

Eating fish regularly may help your emotional well-being. Fish oil—a wonder straight from the Creator—is known for its many benefits as an antioxidant; it is also a weapon against depression and bipolar disorder.

Variations

- Use almonds or peanuts instead of pecans.

- Instead of the tilapia, use another flaky white fish, such as cod.

- Instead of the tilapia, use 1 pound boneless, skinless chicken breasts, cut into strips. Bake for 15 to 18 minutes.

- For crispier fish, fry in olive oil over medium-high heat on the stovetop for about 4 minutes per side.

Basic Cooked Chicken

Makes 4 servings.

1 garlic clove

_____

3 tablespoons extra virgin olive oil
1 tablespoon wine vinegar (red or white)
Scant ¼ teaspoon salt
Several generous grindings of pepper

OPTIONAL INGREDIENTS
- Lemon juice
- Dijon mustard
- Dried herbs (such as parsley, basil, oregano, dill or cumin)
- Small diced onion

_____

1 pound boneless, skinless chicken breasts

1. Chop the garlic.

2. Combine the first five ingredients (garlic through pepper) and any optional ingredients in an 8 x 8-inch baking pan.

3. Wash the chicken and pat dry. Place the chicken in the baking pan and spoon the marinade over the chicken. Cover and refrigerate at least 30 minutes or overnight.

4. When you are ready to cook the chicken, choose a cooking technique:

   a. For baked chicken, preheat the oven to 400 degrees. Cover and bake the chicken for 20 to 30 minutes, until the chicken is cooked through and an instant-read thermometer reads 170 degrees.

   b. For grilled chicken,

      i. Brush the grill lightly with oil and preheat the grill to medium-low.

      ii. Remove the chicken from the marinade and place on the grill.

      iii. Grill for about 5 to 10 minutes per side. (Cooking times will vary with each grill and depend on the size of your chicken breasts.)

 Variations

- To simplify the cooking, skip the seasonings and steam or boil the chicken. These techniques are ideal for *Chicken Salad with Pecans and Grapes* (page 75) or *Turkey Pot Pie* (page 84).

- Use ¼ cup *Lemon Vinaigrette* (page 25), bottled Italian dressing or other vinaigrette as the marinade.

- Spread raw chicken breasts with *Pesto* (page 33) and bake according to step 4a.

Love Thy Leftovers

Use leftover Basic Cooked Chicken instead of raw chicken to prepare *Chicken and Rice Soup with Spinach* (page 120).

Chicken Salad with Pecans and Grapes

If you are pressed for time, use a store-bought rotisserie chicken instead of cooking your own.

Makes 4 servings.

SALAD

1 pound boneless, skinless chicken breasts (or 2 to 3 cups cooked, chopped chicken)

½ cup pecans

2 celery stalks

1 cup red or green grapes

POPPY SEED DRESSING

¼ cup mayonnaise

¼ cup plain yogurt

1 teaspoon poppy seeds

2 teaspoons apple cider vinegar

1 tablespoon honey

¼ teaspoon salt

Several generous grindings of pepper

1. Cook the chicken according to the directions for *Basic Cooked Chicken* (page 74), omitting the garlic and using any cooking method (boiling or steaming is easiest). Allow the chicken to cool before mixing with the remaining ingredients.

2. While the chicken cooks or cools:

   a. Coarsely chop the pecans; chop the celery; and, if desired, cut the grapes in half.

   b. Combine the pecans, celery and grapes in a medium bowl, cover, and refrigerate until the chicken is cool.

   c. Prepare the dressing: combine the dressing ingredients in a small glass jar and shake well, or whisk together in a small bowl.

3. When the chicken is cool, chop into small pieces and add to the bowl with the grape mixture. Add enough of the dressing to evenly coat the chicken (you might not need all of it) and mix to incorporate. Add additional salt if needed.

 Divine Design: Grapes

Helping you breathe easier, God filled grapes with an anti-inflammatory called resveratrol. It soothes your air passageways and prevents lung cancer, while helping to treat asthmatic symptoms. Now that's worth a deep sigh of relief!

Variations

⊙ Experiment with different proportions of mayonnaise and yogurt.

⊙ Substitute 1 medium chopped apple or ½ cup dried cherries or blueberries for the grapes.

⊙ Substitute walnuts for the pecans; add ¼ cup golden raisins to the salad; or add 1 to 2 tablespoons finely chopped onion.

 Love Thy Leftovers

Toss any leftover dressing with a green salad, or use it in place of the dressing for *Classic Coleslaw* (page 5).

Chicken with Peanut Sauce

This dish is similar to the chicken saté served in Thai restaurants.

Makes 6 servings.

1-inch piece of fresh ginger
2 lemon grass stalks

3 garlic cloves
¼ medium red onion

3 tablespoons extra virgin olive oil
2 tablespoons honey
Scant ¼ teaspoon cayenne pepper
½ teaspoon salt
Juice of ½ lemon (about 2 tablespoons)
½ cup peanut butter (creamy or crunchy)

Up to ⅓ cup warm water

1½ pounds boneless, skinless chicken
  breasts

Paprika

1. Peel the ginger. Remove the hard, outer shell, tough stems and any green tops from the lemon grass. Chop the lemon grass into 1-inch pieces.

2. In a food processor or blender, combine the first four ingredients (ginger through onion) and puree until finely chopped.

3. Add the next six ingredients (olive oil through peanut butter) to the food processor and puree until a thick paste is formed.

4. If needed, slowly add the water to obtain the desired consistency. Add additional salt to taste.

5. Wash and pat dry the chicken breasts.

6. If time permits, place the chicken in a 9 x 13-inch baking pan or plastic zipper bag along with several tablespoons of the peanut sauce. Refrigerate for 30 minutes or overnight. Reserve the remaining peanut sauce for a dipping sauce for the cooked chicken.

7. When you are ready to cook the chicken, preheat the oven to 400 degrees.

8. Place the marinated chicken in a 9 x 13-inch baking pan. If you did not marinate it, spread several tablespoons of the peanut sauce over the chicken. Cover and bake for 20 to 30 minutes, until the chicken is cooked through and an instant-read thermometer reads 170 degrees.

9. Lightly sprinkle the cooked chicken with paprika, and serve with the reserved peanut sauce on the side.

 Variations

Serve the chicken over 8 ounces cooked soba noodles tossed with ½ cup peanut sauce, several dashes of sesame oil and salt and pepper to taste.

 Love Thy Leftovers

Toss leftover peanut sauce with steamed broccoli or other steamed vegetables.

Mustard Herb Chicken

Makes 4 servings.

1 to 2 garlic cloves

¼ cup Dijon mustard

2 tablespoons extra virgin olive oil

Juice of ½ lemon (about 2 tablespoons)

1 to 1½ teaspoons dried herbs (any combination of basil, oregano, thyme, rosemary, parsley)

Several generous grindings of pepper

1 pound boneless, skinless chicken breasts

1. Chop the garlic and combine with the next five ingredients (mustard through pepper) in an 8 x 8-inch baking pan.

2. Wash the chicken and pat dry.

3. Place the chicken in the baking pan, and spoon the marinade over the chicken. Cover and refrigerate at least 30 minutes or overnight.

4. When you are ready to cook the chicken, remove it from the refrigerator and preheat the oven to 400 degrees.

5. Cover and bake for about 20 to 30 minutes, until the chicken is cooked through and an instant-read thermometer reads 170 degrees.

Divine Design: Chicken

Where do you get your energy? Instead of reaching for a cup of coffee or a candy bar, consider reaching for a chicken breast. The vitamin B6 found in chicken helps boost your energy the Creator's way by supporting your body's metabolism.

 Variations

- Grill the chicken instead of baking. See *Basic Cooked Chicken* (page 74) for instructions.
- Use fresh herbs instead of dried herbs (1 tablespoon fresh for every 1 teaspoon dried).
- Add 2 to 4 teaspoons capers in step 1.

Asian Chicken

Cucumber Salad (page 12) makes a tasty side dish for Asian Chicken.

Makes 6 servings.

1 garlic clove
1-inch piece of fresh ginger

¼ cup soy sauce
2 tablespoons extra virgin olive oil
1 tablespoon honey
1 tablespoon Dijon mustard

1½ pounds boneless, skinless chicken
  breasts

1. Finely chop the garlic. Peel the ginger (if using) and finely chop or grate it.

2. Combine the garlic and ginger with the next four ingredients (soy sauce through mustard) in a 9 x 13-inch baking pan.

3. Wash and pat dry the chicken breasts.

4. Place the chicken in the baking pan and spoon the marinade over the chicken. Cover and refrigerate at least 30 minutes or overnight.

5. When you are ready to cook the chicken, preheat the oven to 400 degrees.

6. Cover and bake the chicken in a 9 x 13-inch baking pan for 20 to 30 minutes, until the chicken is cooked through and an instant-read thermometer reads 170 degrees.

Divine Design: Ginger

If you suffer from migraines, God's remedy for these ailments might surprise you. By blocking the chemicals that cause inflammation of the blood vessels in your brain, ginger can help keep the pain away.

Variations

◉ Grill the chicken. See *Basic Cooked Chicken* (page 74) for instructions.

◉ Replace the marinade with ¼ cup soy sauce and the juice of 1½ to 2 limes (3 to 4 tablespoons).

◉ Use tuna, halibut or salmon instead of the chicken, and bake according to the directions for *Apricot-Glazed Tuna* (page 69).

 Love Thy Leftovers

◉ Cut leftover Asian Chicken into cubes and add to *Fried Rice* (page 99) to turn a meatless main into a meat dish.

◉ Sauté chopped vegetables in olive oil. Add cubes of leftover Asian Chicken and continue cooking until heated through. Serve over *Basic Cooked Rice* (page 39).

Chicken with Peanut and Coconut Crust

Makes 4 servings.

½ cup oat flour
1½ teaspoons salt
Several generous grindings of pepper
Dash of cayenne pepper

1 egg white
2 tablespoons milk or rice milk

½ cup peanuts
½ cup shredded coconut

1 pound boneless, skinless chicken breasts

1. Preheat the oven to 400 degrees and lightly oil a 9 x 13-inch baking pan.

2. Using 3 shallow bowls or 3 plates:

   a. Combine the flour, salt, pepper and cayenne in the first bowl or plate.

   b. Beat the egg white and combine with the milk in the second bowl or plate.

   c. Finely chop the peanuts and combine with the coconut in the third bowl or plate.

3. Wash the chicken breasts and pat dry. Cut the breasts into strips, 1 to 2 inches wide.

4. For each piece of chicken:

   a. Dredge in the flour mixture, lightly coating both sides.

   b. Dip in the egg mixture, wetting both sides.

   c. Dredge both sides in the peanut mixture.

5. Place the coated chicken pieces in the prepared baking pan. Bake uncovered for 15 to 18 minutes, until the chicken is cooked through and an instant-read thermometer reads 170 degrees.

Variations

- Use almonds instead of peanuts.

- Increase or decrease the amount of peanuts or coconut to suit your taste.

- For crispier chicken, fry in olive oil over medium-high heat on the stovetop for about 5 minutes per side.

- Instead of the chicken, use 1 pound of tilapia. Bake for 12 to 15 minutes.

Roasted Chicken

If you are using a larger chicken, adjust the cooking time: for every pound over 3 pounds, add 15 minutes to the total cooking time.

Makes about 4 servings.

2 garlic cloves
2 tablespoons extra virgin olive oil
2 tablespoons soy sauce
Several generous grindings of pepper
1 sprig of fresh rosemary (optional)

1 whole chicken (about 3 pounds)

2 unpeeled carrots (optional)
1 onion (optional)

1. Preheat the oven to 400 degrees.

2. Chop or crush the garlic. In a small bowl combine the garlic, olive oil, soy sauce and pepper. If using rosemary, remove the leaves from the sprig and add to the garlic mixture. Mix to incorporate.

3. Remove the giblet package from inside the breast cavity of the chicken and discard. Wash the chicken and pat dry.

4. Place the chicken in a roasting pan, breast side up.

5. Using your hand, lift the skin that covers the chicken's breast. Dip your other hand into the garlic mixture and rub a generous amount onto the breast under the skin. Do this for both breasts and the outside of the chicken. (If you prefer, simply rub the garlic mixture over the skin of the entire chicken.)

6. If using, slice the carrots and onion into large chunks and add to the roasting pan.

7. Bake, uncovered, for 45 to 55 minutes, or until an instant-read thermometer inserted into the breast reads 170 degrees.

Divine Design: Chicken

Is eating chicken God's way of keeping you young? Perhaps. A recent study found that eating foods rich in niacin, such as chicken, helps protect people from Alzheimer's disease and other age-related mental declines.

Variations

- Combine 1 teaspoon dried rosemary, 1 teaspoon dried thyme, 1 teaspoon dried basil and 1 chopped garlic clove with enough olive oil to make a thick paste. Spread the mixture over the chicken as described in step 5.

- Instead of spreading the garlic mixture on and under the chicken skin, add the following to the chicken's cavity: 1 small lemon, halved; 2 peeled garlic cloves; and 1 sprig of fresh rosemary. Sprinkle the outside with salt and pepper before roasting.

- Roast chunks of zucchini, red bell peppers or potatoes, in addition to (or in place of) the carrots and onion.

- Follow the same directions to prepare a turkey instead of a chicken. Adjust the cooking temperature and time according to package instructions. Depending on the size of your bird, you may need to increase the garlic mixture ingredients.

Love Thy Leftovers

- Use leftover chicken for *Turkey Pot Pie* (page 84), *Chicken Salad with Pecans and Grapes* (page 75), *Quesadillas* (page 111) or *Mix and Match Salad* (page 10).

- To make your own chicken stock, add the chicken carcass to a large stockpot, cover it with water, and add carrots, onions and fresh parsley. Bring to a boil and simmer for 1½ hours. After it cools, remove the carcass, skim the fat, and freeze the stock for later use.

Sweet Balsamic Chicken

Serve this chicken dish and its juices over cooked rice or millet.

Makes 4 servings.

1 medium onion
1 garlic clove
¼ cup almonds
¼ cup raisins

1 pound boneless, skinless chicken thighs

½ cup balsamic vinegar
¼ cup wine (red or white)
1 tablespoon extra virgin olive oil
1 tablespoon honey
½ teaspoon dried oregano

1. Slice the onion, chop the garlic, and coarsely chop the almonds. Combine them with the raisins in an 8 x 8-inch baking pan.

2. Wash the chicken and pat dry. Spread the chicken over the onion mixture.

3. In a glass measuring cup mix together the remaining ingredients, pour evenly over the chicken breasts, and cover with foil.

4. Refrigerate at least 30 minutes or overnight.

5. When you are ready to cook the chicken, preheat the oven to 400 degrees.

6. Cover and bake for 20 to 30 minutes, until the chicken is cooked though and an instant-read thermometer reads 170 degrees.

 Variations

⊚ Use boneless, skinless chicken breasts instead of thighs.

⊚ Use a thinly sliced small apple instead of or in addition to the raisins.

Tandoori Chicken

Makes 4 servings.

1-inch piece of fresh ginger (or ½ teaspoon ground ginger)

2 garlic cloves

½ medium onion

½ cup plain yogurt

1 tablespoon curry powder

1 teaspoon paprika

1 teaspoon ground coriander

1 teaspoon ground cumin

½ teaspoon salt

½ teaspoon chili powder

Several generous grindings of pepper

Juice of 1 lemon or 2 limes (about ¼ cup)

1 pound boneless, skinless chicken breasts

1. Peel and finely chop or grate the ginger. Chop the garlic and onion. Combine with the remaining ingredients (except the chicken) in an 8 x 8-inch baking pan.

2. Wash the chicken breasts and pat dry.

3. Place the chicken in the baking dish, and spoon the marinade over the chicken. Cover and refrigerate at least 30 minutes or overnight.

4. When you are ready to cook the chicken, preheat the oven to 400 degrees.

5. Cover and bake the chicken for 20 to 30 minutes, until the chicken is cooked through and an instant-read thermometer reads 170 degrees.

 Divine Design: Yogurt

The design of yogurt is full of surprises. It can act as a natural laxative and it can put the stop to diarrhea. The healthy bacteria found in yogurt normalize the imbalanced bacteria in your body, creating this leveling effect.

Variations

⊙ Grill the chicken instead of baking. See *Basic Cooked Chicken* (page 74) for instructions.

⊙ Use any flaky white fish instead of the chicken. Bake at 400 degrees for 12 to 15 minutes, or until the fish flakes easily with a fork.

⊙ Sprinkle chopped cilantro over the chicken before serving.

⊙ Use ½ cup coconut milk in addition to the yogurt.

Love Thy Leftovers

Use leftover chicken in a *Mix and Match Salad* (page 10).

Turkey Pot Pie

This recipe is perfect for Thanksgiving leftovers or store-bought rotisserie chicken. If you don't have either, simply prepare *Basic Cooked Chicken* (page 74).

Makes 6 servings.

FILLING

1 large onion

3 garlic cloves

Extra virgin olive oil

½ cup whole wheat, whole spelt or oat flour

4 cups chicken or vegetable broth

3 unpeeled carrots

3 celery stalks

Heaping ½ teaspoon dried sage

Heaping ½ teaspoon dried thyme

Heaping ½ teaspoon salt

Several generous grindings of pepper

2 to 3 cups frozen vegetables (any combination of green beans, corn and peas)

3 to 4 cups diced cooked turkey or chicken (1 to 1½ pounds)

BISCUIT TOPPING

2 cups whole wheat or whole spelt flour

¼ cup cornmeal or corn flour

4 teaspoons baking powder

½ teaspoon baking soda

Heaping ¼ teaspoon salt

½ cup extra virgin olive oil

⅔ cup kefir or plain yogurt

1. Prepare the filling:

   a. Chop the onion and garlic.

   b. Coat the bottom of a stockpot with olive oil (about 2 tablespoons) and sauté the onion and garlic over medium-high heat.

   c. When the onion is soft, add the flour to the pot and mix to incorporate. Continue cooking for 2 minutes. Add the broth and whisk to break up any lumps.

   d. Chop the carrots and celery and add to the pot. Continue cooking over medium heat for about 15 minutes. The filling mixture should begin to thicken and be slowly boiling during this time.

   e. Add the sage, thyme, salt and pepper and continue cooking for an additional 5 minutes.

   f. Add the frozen vegetables and turkey. Continue cooking until all the ingredients are well heated. Lower the heat to keep the filling warm while making the topping.

2. Preheat the oven to 425 degrees.

3. Prepare the Biscuit Topping:

   a. In a medium bowl combine the dry ingredients (flour through salt) and mix to incorporate.

   b. In a separate small bowl combine the wet ingredients (olive oil and kefir). Mix to incorporate.

   c. Pour the wet ingredients into the dry ingredients. Mix to incorporate.

4. Pour the filling mixture into a 9 x 13-inch baking pan (if the pan is very full, place it on top of a cookie sheet).

5. Drop equal-sized pieces of topping dough evenly across the top of the filling. (The dough will expand to cover much of the surface area.)

6. Bake for 15 to 20 minutes, or until the topping is slightly browned and the filling is bubbling.

Divine Design: Turkey

The dark meat of turkey and other poultry, though somewhat higher in fat than white meat, was still created by God. Dark meat actually contains nearly three times as much calcium as white meat, and almost twice the iron.

Variation

⊛ Instead of preparing the biscuit topping, place several sheets of phyllo dough over the top of the filling.

⊛ For softer vegetables, sauté the carrots and celery with the onion and garlic in step 1b rather than adding them during step 1d.

Turkey Sausage

Don't let the looks of this sausage fool you! Although not a traditional sausage patty or link made in casing, this crumbled sausage can be used as an Italian-style sausage in *Mix and Match Whole Grain Pasta* (page 46), *Quiche* (page 113), *Millet Casserole* (page 49) or *Meat Chili* (page 133). Keep in mind that ground turkey from dark meat makes a juicier sausage than ground turkey from white meat.

Makes 4 servings.

1 pound ground turkey

¾ teaspoon salt

Several generous grindings of pepper (about ½ teaspoon)

½ teaspoon whole fennel seeds

Heaping ½ teaspoon dried basil

Heaping ½ teaspoon dried oregano

Scant ¼ teaspoon cayenne pepper

1. Thoroughly combine all of the ingredients in a medium bowl.

2. Using a nonstick frying pan (or a lightly oiled regular pan), cook the meat mixture over medium heat. Stir frequently, breaking up the meat pieces with a wooden spoon. The meat is cooked when it is no longer pink.

 Variation

For breakfast sausages, substitute 1½ teaspoons dried sage for the basil, oregano and cayenne pepper, and use ½ teaspoon ground fennel instead of the whole fennel seeds. Shape the meat into approximately 6 patties or links, and cook over medium heat until they are lightly browned on all sides and no longer pink on the inside.

 Love Thy Leftovers

If you don't think you're going to eat an entire batch of Turkey Sausage, season and cook the entire pound and freeze it for later use in a plastic container or a freezer bag. Thaw before reheating.

Beef Brisket

The keys to tender brisket are baking at a low temperature, making sure the meat is mostly submerged in liquid and cooking the meat long enough.

Makes 8 servings.

1 medium onion

2 garlic cloves

1 cup red wine

1 cup soy sauce or tamari, plus additional for cooking

Several generous grindings of pepper

2 pounds beef brisket

1. Chop the onion and garlic, and combine with the wine, soy sauce and pepper in an ovenproof pot with a tight-fitting lid, such as a Dutch oven.

2. Trim the visible excess fat off the brisket. Place the brisket in the wine mixture (it is OK to cut the brisket in half to fit the pot), and refrigerate for at least 2 hours or overnight.

3. When you are ready to cook the brisket, preheat the oven to 300 degrees.

4. If needed, add additional soy sauce, water, broth or any combination to make sure that most of the brisket is submerged in liquid.

5. Cover the pot and bake for 2 hours (reduce cooking time to 1½ hours if you cut your brisket in half).

6. Remove the brisket from the pot, and reserve the liquid in the pot. Slice the entire brisket against the grain. If it is not tender, return the sliced meat to the liquid-filled pot and continue cooking for another 30 minutes or more, until the meat is very tender.

7. Serve the brisket with the hot reserved liquid as gravy.

Divine Design: Beef

Cattle that have been fed animal byproducts (thereby circumventing God's design for bovine vegetarianism) pose the risk of transmitting mad cow disease to humans. However, lean organic beef—fully cooked and eaten in a balanced diet—protects the heart and can prevent colon cancer.

 Variations

Add additional onion, carrot or potato chunks to the pot after 1 hour of baking.

Gyros

Serve gyros in whole grain pita pockets with chopped tomatoes and onions, topped with tzatziki sauce. Or serve over a bed of greens or a bed of rice topped with the sauce.

Makes about 4 servings.

GYROS

⅓ bunch parsley (mostly leaves)
5 garlic cloves
½ medium onion
1 heaping teaspoon dried oregano
Juice of ¼ lemon (about 1 tablespoon)
½ to 1 teaspoon salt
Several generous grindings of pepper
½ pound lean ground lamb
½ pound lean ground beef

TZATZIKI SAUCE

½ unpeeled medium cucumber
8 to 12 fresh mint leaves
⅛ medium red onion
1 garlic clove
Juice of ¼ lemon (about 1 tablespoon)
1 cup plain yogurt
¼ to ½ teaspoon salt
Several generous grindings of pepper

1. Preheat the oven to 350 degrees. Prepare the gyros:

   a. Finely chop the parsley, garlic and onion. Place the chopped ingredients in a large bowl.

   b. Add the remaining gyros ingredients to the bowl. Using your hands or a fork, thoroughly combine all the ingredients.

2. Divide the meat mixture in half and shape into two 1½-inch-thick loaves. Place the loaves into an 8 x 8-inch baking pan. Bake for about 30 minutes, or until the meat is no longer pink. While the gyros cook, prepare the tzatziki sauce:

   a. If desired, seed the cucumber to help keep the sauce fresh longer.

   b. Finely chop the cucumber, mint, red onion and garlic. Place the chopped ingredients in a medium bowl.

   c. Add the remaining tzatziki sauce ingredients to the bowl and thoroughly combine.

3. Once the gyros are cooked, cool slightly and cut into ¼-inch slices before serving.

 Variations

- Use lamb stew meat and beef stew meat instead of the ground meats. Finely chop the meats in the food processor. Add the remaining gyros ingredients to the food processor and finely chop.

- For a creamier sauce, combine all the sauce ingredients in a blender or food processor.

- Substitute 1 teaspoon dried dill for the mint in the sauce.

- To grill the gyros instead of baking, shape the meat mixture into four square-shaped patties and grill until no longer pink.

Love Thy Leftovers

Use leftover tzatziki sauce on either version of *Veggie Burgers* (pages 108 and 109), or toss with a mixed green salad.

Meat Loaf

If you use ground turkey, you will have a slightly drier loaf than with beef, especially if you use white meat.

Makes 4 servings.

2 slices whole grain bread

1½ teaspoons dried parsley

¼ teaspoon salt

½ teaspoon dried oregano

1 tablespoon Parmesan cheese (optional)

1 medium onion

1 garlic clove

1 pound lean ground beef, ground turkey or a combination

⅔ cup milk or rice milk

1 egg, slightly beaten

2 tablespoons Dijon mustard

1 tablespoon Worcestershire sauce

Several generous grindings of pepper

3 tablespoons ketchup (optional)

1. Preheat the oven to 350 degrees.

2. Tear the bread into pieces and place into a food processor or blender. Process until the bread becomes bread crumbs and add to a large bowl. Mix in the parsley, salt, oregano and Parmesan cheese.

3. Finely chop the onion and garlic and add to the bowl.

4. Add the next six ingredients (ground beef through pepper) to the bowl. Using your hands or a fork, thoroughly combine the ingredients.

5. Place the meat mixture in a loaf pan, or shape the mixture into a loaf and place on an 8 x 8-inch baking pan.

6. Spread a thin layer of ketchup over the top of the loaf and bake, uncovered, for 1 hour. Cool slightly before cutting into slices.

Divine Design: Beef

Going vegan may pose some risks. A truly balanced diet includes vitamin B12. Found almost exclusively in meat, eggs and dairy products, this essential vitamin protects your nervous system, prevents Alzheimer's disease and is needed for your cells to divide properly. Beef is a fabulous source of this necessary vitamin.

Variations

⊙ Use ½ cup whole grain bread crumbs instead of the bread, and then add the seasonings listed.

⊙ Use up to ½ pound ground lamb in place of the beef or turkey.

⊙ Add 1 finely diced carrot or up to ½ bunch finely chopped fresh parsley to the meat loaf.

Old-Fashioned Meat Sauce

Meat sauce is not just for pasta anymore. It can also be served over cooked millet, brown rice or the crust from *Polenta Pizza* (page 52).

Makes about 3 quarts.

2 medium onions
2 to 4 garlic cloves
Extra virgin olive oil

1 pound lean ground beef, ground turkey
  or a combination

1, 14-ounce can chopped tomatoes,
  undrained
1, 15-ounce can tomato sauce
2, 6-ounce cans tomato paste
1½ cups water, broth or tomato juice
2 teaspoons dried parsley
2 teaspoons dried basil
2 teaspoons dried oregano
1½ to 2 teaspoons salt
Several generous grindings of pepper

1. Chop the onions and garlic.

2. Coat the bottom of a stockpot with olive oil (about 2 tablespoons) and sauté the onions and garlic over medium-high heat.

3. Add the ground meat and cook until mostly browned, about 10 minutes. (During this time, stir the meat frequently to break up any pieces.)

4. Add the remaining ingredients and bring to a boil. Turn the heat to low and simmer, uncovered, for about 1 hour, stirring occasionally.

Divine Design: Beef

Cows were crafted by God to be ruminants—animals that chew their cud. Their complex digestive systems include multiple stomachs that thoroughly process food and remove toxins before they are absorbed into the meat you eat. God certainly knew what He was doing when He declared ruminants "clean."

Variations

⊙ To prepare the meat sauce in a slow cooker, cook for 5 to 7 hours on low heat, stirring occasionally.

⊙ Use up to ½ pound ground lamb in place of the beef or turkey.

Tamale Pie

When you prepare the filling it might appear too soupy, but do not drain the tomatoes or beans—the end product will turn out fine!

Makes 6 servings.

FILLING

1 large onion

1 tablespoon extra virgin olive oil

1 pound lean ground beef or turkey (or a combination)

1½ cups chopped vegetables (any combination of carrots, green peppers or frozen corn)

2 teaspoons chili powder

1 teaspoon ground cumin

1 teaspoon salt

1, 15-ounce can of black beans, undrained

1, 28-ounce can of diced tomatoes, undrained

Several generous grindings of pepper

CORNBREAD TOPPING

1 cup flour (whole wheat, whole spelt, oat or a combination)

1 cup cornmeal or corn flour

1½ teaspoons baking powder

½ teaspoon baking soda

Heaping ¼ teaspoon salt

1 cup kefir or plain yogurt

¼ cup extra virgin olive oil

2 eggs

1. Chop the onion and sauté in the olive oil in a large frying pan over medium-high heat until soft, about 5 minutes. Add the meat and cook until browned.

2. Chop the vegetables, add to the pan, and sauté until they begin to soften, about 5 minutes.

3. Add the remaining filling ingredients to the pan and mix to incorporate.

4. Pour the filling ingredients into a 9 x 13-inch baking pan and set aside.

5. Preheat the oven to 350 degrees.

6. In a medium bowl combine the cornbread topping dry ingredients (flour through salt).

7. In a glass measuring cup, mix the cornbread topping wet ingredients (kefir through eggs).

8. Pour the wet ingredients into the dry ingredients and mix to incorporate.

9. Spread the cornbread mixture evenly over the filling in the pan, making sure to completely cover the filling.

10. Bake, uncovered, for about 45 minutes, or until the cornbread topping is golden brown.

 Variation

Experiment with different filling ingredients, such as sliced black olives or diced jalapeños.

Vietnamese Beef Salad

Serving the vegetables separately from the meat and noodles (or rice) prevents the vegetables from getting soggy and makes for better leftovers. If you prefer to toss them all together, that works too.

Makes about 4 servings.

MEAT

1 pound flank, skirt or sirloin steak

Sesame oil or extra virgin olive oil

SAUCE

1 small red onion

1-inch piece of fresh ginger

¼ cup soy sauce

Juice of ½ lime (about 1 tablespoon)

1 tablespoon sesame oil

2 tablespoons fish sauce (optional)

VEGETABLES

20 to 30 fresh basil leaves (about ¼ cup firmly packed)

⅓ bunch cilantro (mostly leaves)

2 unpeeled carrots

1 zucchini

NOODLES OR RICE

8 ounces cooked rice noodles or 3 cups cooked brown rice

OPTIONAL TOPPINGS

- Bean sprouts
- Chopped peanuts
- Chopped cucumber
- Chopped red or green cabbage

1. Thinly cut the steak into bite-sized pieces.

2. Coat the bottom of a frying pan with oil (about 2 tablespoons) and sauté the steak over medium-high heat until no longer pink.

3. Drain any extra liquid or fat from the meat and set aside.

4. Make the sauce:

   a. Chop the onion.

   b. Peel the ginger and grate or finely chop.

   c. Combine the onion and ginger with the remaining sauce ingredients in a small bowl.

5. Prepare the vegetables:

   a. Finely chop the basil and cilantro. Set aside.

   b. Grate or finely chop the carrots and zucchini. Set aside.

6. Combine the cooked noodles (best if warm) or rice with the steak and sauce in a large bowl. Mix to incorporate.

7. Serve the noodle (or rice) and meat mixture topped with the vegetables and optional toppings.

Chapter 4
Meatless Main Dishes

Rice Salad with Garbanzo Beans, Dill and Feta

Red Bean and Rice Salad with Lime Dressing

Fried Rice

Green Curry with Black Beans and Rice

Garbanzo Bean Curry

Lentil Loaf with Cashew Sauce

Lentil Salad

Refried Bean Wraps

Sweet Potato and Black Bean Burritos

Veggie Burgers with Garbanzo Beans and Walnuts

Veggie Burgers with Millet and Sweet Potatoes

Quinoa with Feta, Capers and Sun-Dried Tomatoes

Quesadillas

Egg Salad

Quiche

Meatless mains are not just for vegetarians! We are not vegetarians, but we have boosted our intake of the plant-based proteins God gave us by eating more meatless main dishes than we have in the past. By doing so, we have reduced our grocery bills; increased the fiber, vitamins and antioxidants in our diets; and provided a wide variety of meals to our families.

Of the nonmeat protein sources, beans are the champions. High in fiber and taste, low in cost and fat, beans are clearly a gift from God. Of course, He provided dried beans (rather than canned beans), but our recipes use canned in order to speed preparation. In a perfect world, we would be using dried (which usually need to be picked over, soaked and cooked before using them). If you use dried beans instead of canned in our recipes, use a good conversion chart to determine the quantity to use, since dried beans expand quite a bit after they are cooked.

Are you thinking about going completely meatless? According to Dr. Russell, if you choose to follow a vegetarian or vegan diet, you run a high risk of vitamin B12 deficiency. If you are thinking about becoming a vegetarian or vegan, be sure to do your homework to ensure that you are not missing this very important God-given nutrient.

A final note: Some variations and leftover ideas for these recipes suggest adding meat or fish. In their basic form, however, all the recipes in this chapter are indeed vegetarian, as long as you use vegetable broth rather than chicken broth where indicated.

Principle 1

Beans, grains, eggs, nuts and cheese—they are all packed with God-given protein and other nutrients. What a Creator! He provided plenty of nonmeat protein sources that are delicious and easy to prepare.

Principle 2

Do not be deceived. Store-bought "meat substitutes" are man-made and are no substitute for God's protein sources. Keep meatless meals simple and pure—close to God's original design.

Principle 3

Try a few meatless lunches and dinners each week. God's satisfying nonmeat protein sources will help curb the desire for eating meat at every meal.

Rice Salad with Garbanzo Beans, Dill and Feta

Makes about 6 cups.

1 cup brown rice
2 cups chicken or vegetable broth

3 green onions (white and some green)
5 to 6 sprigs of fresh dill
¼ red onion
1 garlic clove

1, 15-ounce can of garbanzo beans, rinsed and drained

2 ounces feta cheese

3 tablespoons extra virgin olive oil
Juice of 1 lemon (about ¼ cup)
½ teaspoon salt
Several generous grindings of pepper

1. Prepare the rice with the broth according to the directions for *Basic Cooked Rice* (page 39), omitting the optional seasonings.

2. While the rice is cooking:

   a. Finely chop the green onions, dill, red onion and garlic, and add to a large bowl.

   b. Rinse and drain the garbanzo beans and add to the bowl.

   c. Crumble the feta cheese with a fork and add to the bowl.

   d. Add the remaining ingredients to the bowl and mix to incorporate.

3. When the rice is done, transfer it to the bowl and toss lightly. (Allow the rice to cool if you want the feta to remain a little chunky; otherwise it will melt from the rice's heat.)

4. Serve at room temperature.

Divine Design: Garbanzo Beans

If you want to find new plant-based sources of protein, look no further than garbanzo beans. When paired with a grain such as brown rice, you get the benefit of a high-protein, high-fiber meal that's low in fat.

 Variation

Add a diced roasted red pepper to the salad.

 Love Thy Leftovers

Add a can of tuna (drained and flaked) to the leftover rice salad. Add additional lemon juice, olive oil and salt to taste.

Red Bean and Rice Salad with Lime Dressing

Makes about 6 cups.

SALAD

⅔ cup brown rice

1⅓ cups chicken or vegetable broth

(Or 2 cups cooked brown rice)

1½ cups grape or cherry tomatoes

½ red bell pepper

4 green onions (white and some green)

¼ medium red onion

⅓ bunch cilantro (mostly leaves)

½ jalapeño, seeded (optional)

½ cup frozen corn, thawed

1, 15-ounce can of kidney beans, rinsed and drained

LIME DRESSING

Juice of 1½ limes (about 3 tablespoons)

1 tablespoon extra virgin olive oil

2 tablespoons balsamic vinegar

¼ to ½ teaspoon salt

¼ teaspoon ground cumin

Dash of cayenne pepper

Several generous grindings of pepper

1. Prepare the rice with the broth according to the directions for *Basic Cooked Rice* (page 39), omitting any optional seasonings.

2. While the rice is cooking:

    a. Halve the tomatoes and chop the pepper and green onions and add to a large bowl.

    b. Finely chop the cilantro and jalapeño (if using) and add to the bowl. Add the corn.

    c. Rinse and drain the beans and add to the bowl.

    d. Prepare the dressing by combining the dressing ingredients in a small glass jar and shaking well, or whisk together in a small bowl.

3. When the rice is finished cooking, cool slightly and toss with the vegetables and the dressing. Serve cold or at room temperature.

 Variations

- Substitute black beans for the kidney beans.

- Top individual portions with sliced olives or avocado just before serving.

- Add a chopped carrot or a diced cucumber to the salad.

- Experiment by substituting barley or other whole grains for the rice.

Fried Rice

You can use leftover brown rice to make this dish, which is great for breakfast, lunch or dinner.

Makes about 5 cups.

2 garlic cloves

3 green onions (white and some green) or ½ small onion

2-inch piece of fresh ginger

2 cups mixed, chopped vegetables, such as:

- Peas
- Corn
- Unpeeled carrots
- Broccoli
- Green beans (1-inch pieces)
- Sugar snap peas
- Bean sprouts
- Zucchini

1 to 2 tablespoons sesame oil (or extra virgin olive oil)

2 cups cooked brown rice (best if refrigerated)

2 eggs

2 to 3 tablespoons soy sauce or tamari

Salt and pepper to taste

1. Chop the garlic and onions. Peel the ginger and finely chop or grate. Chop the vegetables.

2. In a large frying pan heat the sesame oil over medium-high heat. Sauté the garlic, onions and ginger for 2 to 3 minutes. Add the rice. Stir to coat the rice with the garlic mixture and sauté for several more minutes.

3. While the rice is sautéing, prepare the eggs according to the directions for *Basic Scrambled Eggs* (page 152) in a small frying pan. When the eggs are cooked, add to the rice mixture, breaking the eggs into smaller pieces.

4. Add the chopped vegetables and soy sauce to the rice mixture. Continue to cook until everything is mixed and coated and the vegetables are cooked to the desired tenderness.

5. Add salt, pepper and additional soy sauce to taste.

 Divine Design: Eggs

The Creator packed eggs with nutrients, including vitamins B12 (which prevents anemia and fatigue) and D (which prevents rickets). These vitamins cannot be gleaned from purely vegan sources; the most complete forms of these nutrients are found in animal products, such as eggs.

Variation

Add chopped, cooked *Asian Chicken* (page 78) in step 4.

Green Curry with Black Beans and Rice

While the word *curry* is commonly associated with a bottled powdered Indian spice mix, authentic Indian curry powders and curry pastes are freshly prepared blends of a variety of herbs and spices. *Curry* is actually a term for any spicy, saucy dish seasoned with these spice blends.

Makes 4 to 6 servings.

GREEN CURRY PASTE

1 lemon grass stalk

½ medium red onion
2 garlic cloves

¼ to ⅓ bunch cilantro (mostly leaves)
1½ teaspoons ground coriander
½ teaspoon ground cumin
Lots of fresh ground pepper (about ½ teaspoon)
1 tablespoon water
2 tablespoons extra virgin olive oil

2 cups light coconut milk (½ to 1 cup water can be substituted)

BEANS AND RICE

2, 15-ounce cans of black beans, rinsed and drained
½ teaspoon salt
Juice of ½ lime (about 1 tablespoon)

3 cups cooked brown rice

1. Remove the hard outer shell, tough stems and green tops from the lemon grass. Cut into 1-inch pieces, place in a food processor, and finely chop.

2. Add the onion and garlic to the food processor and finely chop.

3. Add the cilantro to the food processor along with the remaining curry paste ingredients. Process until the ingredients are well combined and form a thick paste.

4. In a large frying pan combine the curry paste with the coconut milk, mix to incorporate, and cook over medium heat for 5 to 10 minutes.

5. Rinse and drain the black beans and add to the curry paste and coconut milk mixture. Continue heating for another 5 to 10 minutes, or until the beans and cooking liquid are heated through. Add the salt and lime juice before serving. Serve over the brown rice.

 Variation

Top with green onions and/or cilantro.

Garbanzo Bean Curry

Serve over cooked brown rice or millet.

Makes 5 to 6 servings.

1 large onion

2 garlic cloves

¼ cup extra virgin olive oil

1 tablespoon curry powder

2 tablespoons whole wheat, whole spelt or oat flour

1½ cups chicken or vegetable broth

¼ cup honey

¼ cup tomato paste

2, 15-ounce cans of garbanzo beans, rinsed and drained

Several generous grindings of pepper

Salt to taste

⅓ bunch cilantro (mostly leaves)

1. Chop the onion and garlic, and sauté in the olive oil in a medium saucepan over medium-high heat.

2. Cook until the onion begins to soften, about 5 minutes. Add the curry powder and mix to incorporate. Cook for about 1 minute.

3. Add the flour to the pan and cook for 1 additional minute, stirring to incorporate.

4. Stir in the broth, honey and tomato paste. Reduce the heat to low and continue cooking for 3 to 5 more minutes.

5. Rinse and drain the garbanzo beans and add them to the saucepan. Season with pepper and add salt if needed. Mix to incorporate and cook until thoroughly heated through, 5 to 10 minutes.

6. Chop the cilantro and sprinkle over the bean mixture before serving.

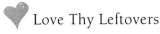 Variations

⊚ Sauté a chopped carrot or zucchini or other chopped vegetables along with the onions and garlic.

⊚ Stir in chopped *Basic Cooked Chicken* (page 74) or chopped *Roasted Chicken* (page 80) in step 5.

Love Thy Leftovers

Toss together leftover Garbanzo Bean Curry and leftover rice, and serve as a side dish for chicken or fish.

Lentil Loaf with Cashew Sauce

Makes 1 loaf.

1 cup green or brown lentils
2½ cups water

½ cup water
½ cup bulgur

2 celery stalks
2 unpeeled carrots
1 onion
Extra virgin olive oil

1 tablespoon dried parsley
1 tablespoon dried sage
1 tablespoon dried thyme
1 tablespoon soy sauce or tamari
1 teaspoon salt
Several generous grindings of pepper

2 cups rolled oats
⅓ cup walnuts
⅓ cup sesame seeds
⅓ cup sunflower seeds

Cashew Sauce (recipe follows)

1. Preheat the oven to 350 degrees and oil a standard loaf pan.

2. Add the lentils and 2½ cups water to a medium saucepan and cook over medium-high heat. Bring to a boil, reduce the heat, and simmer until soft, about 35 minutes. While the lentils cook:

   a. In a small saucepan bring ½ cup water to a boil. Add the bulgur, stir, cover, and remove from the heat.

   b. Finely dice the celery, carrots and onion.

   c. Coat the bottom of a large stockpot with olive oil (about 2 tablespoons) and sauté the vegetables over medium-high heat or until soft.

   d. Add the next six ingredients (parsley through pepper) to the pan. Mix to incorporate and cook for an additional 5 minutes.

   e. In a food processor or blender, pulse the oats 10 to 20 times, until coarsely chopped. Add the walnuts to the oats and pulse again until the nuts are coarsely chopped. Add the oats and nuts to the pan, along with the sesame and sunflower seeds. Mix to incorporate.

3. When the lentils are soft, add them (without draining) to the frying pan, along with the undrained bulgur. (Or combine all the ingredients in a large bowl.) Mix well to incorporate and add up to an additional ½ cup water (if needed) to make the mixture stick together.

4. Transfer the mixture to the prepared pan, pressing the mixture firmly into the pan. Bake, uncovered, for 1 hour. While the lentil loaf cooks, prepare the Cashew Sauce.

5. Cut the lentil loaf into slices and serve with the Cashew Sauce spread over the top or on the side.

❦❦❦❦ Divine Design: Bulgur

This slightly processed version of nutrient-rich and fiber-filled whole wheat is great for preventing and fighting cancer. Lignans—antioxidants God placed in bulgur—protect cells from dangerous changes, while also safeguarding your body from any cancerous cells that might already exist.

Cashew Sauce

Do not clean the pan after you have prepared this sauce! The pan used to cook the onions and garlic in step 2 is perfect for sautéing spinach or Swiss chard during the final minutes of your meal's preparation.

Makes about 2 cups.

2 medium onions
1 garlic clove
Extra virgin olive oil

Heaping ⅓ cup cashew butter
¼ cup soy sauce or tamari

¼ to ½ cup water

1. Coarsely chop the onions and garlic.

2. Coat the bottom of a large frying pan with olive oil (about 2 tablespoons) and sauté the onions and garlic over medium-high heat until they are very soft and begin to brown, about 12 to 15 minutes.

3. Add the onion mixture, cashew butter and soy sauce to a food processor or blender. Puree until smooth.

4. Add 2 tablespoons water to the food processor and process until smooth. Continue adding water, 2 tablespoons at a time, until the sauce reaches the desired flavor and consistency.

5. Transfer the sauce to a small saucepan and simmer over low heat until you are ready to serve. If necessary, add additional water for thinner sauce.

 Variation

Substitute tahini or almond butter for the cashew butter.

 Love Thy Leftovers

⊙ Serve leftover sauce with *Meat Loaf* (page 89).

⊙ Stir leftover sauce into sautéed greens, such as kale or Swiss chard.

Lentil Salad

Makes about 5 cups.

SALAD

2 garlic cloves

1 cup green or brown lentils

½ teaspoon dried thyme

⅓ cup sun-dried tomatoes

½ medium red onion

1 to 2 cups mixed, chopped vegetables, such as:

- ⊛ Red or yellow bell pepper
- ⊛ Unpeeled carrot
- ⊛ Celery stalk

⅓ bunch parsley (mostly leaves; optional)

FENNEL VINAIGRETTE

⅓ cup extra virgin olive oil

3 tablespoons red wine vinegar

1 teaspoon ground fennel

1 heaping teaspoon Dijon mustard

¼ to ½ teaspoon salt

Several generous grindings of pepper

1. Cut the garlic cloves in half and add them to a medium saucepan along with the lentils, thyme and 3 to 4 inches of water. Bring to a boil over medium-high heat.

2. Reduce the heat and simmer, stirring occasionally, for about 20 minutes, until the lentils are tender. While the lentils simmer:

   a. Cover the sun-dried tomatoes with very hot or boiling water and set aside. (If you are using oil-packed sun-dried tomatoes, there is no need to soak them; just shake off the excess oil before using.)

   b. Finely dice the onion, vegetables and parsley (if using) and add to a large bowl.

   c. In a separate bowl whisk the vinaigrette ingredients until smooth.

   d. Once the sun-dried tomatoes have softened (about 10 minutes), drain and mince them and add them to the vegetables.

3. Once the lentils and garlic are soft, drain them in a colander and add to the bowl.

4. Remove the garlic pieces from the lentils, mash the garlic against the side of the bowl, and mix the garlic in with the vegetables and lentils.

5. Toss the lentils and vegetables with the dressing and add additional salt or pepper to taste. Serve at room temperature.

 Variations

- ⊛ Add chopped *Basic Cooked Chicken* (page 74), chopped walnuts or pine nuts to the salad.
- ⊛ Use 1 to 2 cups *Basic Roasted Vegetables* (page 15) instead of the chopped raw vegetables.
- ⊛ Add crumbled feta or goat cheese to the salad.

 Love Thy Leftovers

Double the amount of lentils, garlic and water, and use the extra cooked lentils to add to a *Mix and Match Salad* (page 10).

Refried Bean Wraps

Makes 6 wraps.

REFRIED BEANS

1 medium onion

4 garlic cloves

Extra virgin olive oil

2, 15-ounce cans of pinto beans, rinsed and drained

1 heaping teaspoon dried cumin

¼ to ½ teaspoon salt

Several generous grindings of pepper

Dash of cayenne pepper (optional)

OPTIONAL FILLINGS

- Avocados
- Tomatoes
- Black olives
- Cilantro
- Red or yellow bell pepper
- Fresh spinach

WRAPS

6, 8-inch whole wheat tortillas

2 to 3 tablespoons salsa per wrap

1. Chop the onion and garlic. Coat the bottom of a large frying pan with olive oil (about 2 tablespoons) and sauté the onion and garlic over medium-high heat.

2. While the onion and garlic cook, rinse and drain the beans. When the onion and garlic are soft (about 5 minutes), add the beans to the frying pan and reduce the heat to low.

3. Using a potato masher or fork, mash the beans to obtain a chunky consistency. (Add 2 to 3 tablespoons of water, if needed.) For a creamier consistency, puree the beans in a food processor before adding to the frying pan.

4. Add the cumin, salt, pepper and cayenne (if using). Mix to incorporate and allow the beans to cook for several minutes before serving.

5. As the beans finish heating, dice your choice of optional filling ingredients and briefly heat the tortillas in a separate frying pan, if desired.

6. Scoop up the bean mixture using a heaping ¼-cup measure and spread in the middle of each tortilla. Top with the salsa and fillings of your choices. Roll up the tortillas and serve immediately.

 Variations

- Use black beans instead of pinto beans.
- Use the refried beans in your favorite taco or tostada recipe.
- For a hummus wrap, substitute *Hummus* (page 192) for the refried beans and omit the salsa. Top with your choice of chopped vegetables.

♥ Love Thy Leftovers

Use any leftover refried beans as a dip: stir in prepared salsa and enjoy with vegetables or baked tortilla chips.

Sweet Potato and Black Bean Burritos

This simple recipe is even simpler if you use a food processor (see the variation).

Makes about 6 burritos.

1 unpeeled large sweet potato (about 1 pound)

1 large onion
2 garlic cloves
1 tablespoon extra virgin olive oil

2 teaspoons ground cumin
2 teaspoons ground coriander
½ teaspoon salt
Several generous grindings of pepper

⅓ bunch cilantro (mostly leaves)
2, 15-ounce cans of black beans, rinsed and drained
Juice from ½ lemon or 1 lime (about 2 tablespoons)

6, 8-inch whole wheat tortillas
Shredded cheese (optional)

OPTIONAL TOPPINGS
- Prepared salsa
- *Guacamole* (page 191)

1. Preheat the oven to 400 degrees and oil a 9 x 13-inch baking pan.

2. Cut the potato into chunks and put them on the prepared pan. Bake for 20 minutes, or until the potato pieces are tender when pierced with a fork.

3. While the potato bakes:

   a. Chop the onion and garlic. Sauté in the olive oil over medium-high heat in a large frying pan.

   b. Cook until the onion is soft, about 5 minutes. Add the cumin, coriander, salt and pepper and cook for 2 to 3 more minutes. Remove from the heat.

   c. Chop the cilantro. Rinse and drain the black beans. Add the cilantro, beans and lemon juice to the pan.

4. When the potato chunks are cooked, remove from the oven. Reduce the heat to 350 degrees.

5. Add the cooked potato to the frying pan with the onion mixture. (Set aside the pan you used to bake the potato; you will use it to heat the burritos.) Using a potato masher, mash the ingredients together to make a thick, chunky mixture.

6. To assemble the burritos:

   a. Lay a tortilla on a flat surface. If you are using cheese, sprinkle a small amount over the tortilla.

   b. Spoon ½ cup of the filling mixture over the tortilla.

   c. Roll up the tortilla and place in the pan you used to bake the potato with the seam side down.

   d. Repeat this process for as many burritos as you plan to eat. (Refrigerate or freeze any leftover filling for future use.)

7. Cover the pan with foil and bake the burritos for 30 minutes, until well heated. Serve with salsa and guacamole, if desired.

Divine Design: Sweet Potatoes

Sweet potatoes' antidiabetic effects are amazing. The Creator's plan includes providing this spectacular blood sugar stabilizer that also lowers insulin resistance.

Variations

- For speedier preparation and a smoother filling, use a food processor to chop the onions and garlic (step 3a), to chop the cilantro (step 3c) and to pulse the onion mixture, beans and potato (step 5) until the desired textured is reached. You may need to do this in several batches.

- Add cooked, shredded chicken from *Basic Cooked Chicken* (page 74) at the end of step 5.

Love Thy Leftovers

If you do not use all of the filling, freeze it in an airtight container or freezer bag. Thaw before using in more burritos.

Veggie Burgers with Garbanzo Beans and Walnuts

Serve the burgers in whole wheat pitas with lettuce, chopped tomatoes and *Cucumber Dill Dressing* (page 28) or *Ranch Dressing* (page 29). The consistency of these patties is a bit more crumbly than store-bought frozen patties because we don't use gums or artificial binding ingredients.

Makes about 8, 3-inch burgers.

2 slices whole grain bread
1½ teaspoons dried parsley
¼ teaspoon salt
½ teaspoon dried oregano
1 tablespoon Parmesan cheese (optional)

⅓ bunch cilantro (stems OK)
1 unpeeled carrot
½ medium onion

1, 15-ounce can of garbanzo beans, rinsed and drained
Juice of ½ lime (about 1 tablespoon)
¾ cup walnuts
2 eggs
¼ teaspoon salt
1 heaping teaspoon cumin seeds
Several generous grindings of pepper
1 to 2 tablespoons extra virgin olive oil

1. Preheat the oven to 400 degrees and oil a jelly roll pan (or cookie sheet).

2. Process the bread slices in a food processor until they become bread crumbs. Add the parsley, salt, oregano and Parmesan cheese and pulse to incorporate.

3. Cut off the bottom 1 or 2 inches from the cilantro. Cut the carrot into large chunks and place the carrot, cilantro and onion in the food processor. Pulse until all the vegetables are finely chopped.

4. Rinse and drain the garbanzo beans and add to the food processor along with the remaining ingredients. Pulse until combined. The mixture should be thick and somewhat chunky.

5. Scoop up the veggie burger mixture using a heaping ¼-cup measure and drop onto the prepared pan. Flatten and shape each burger into a patty, about 3 inches in diameter and ¾ inch thick.

6. Bake the veggie burgers for about 20 to 25 minutes, until golden brown.

Divine Design: Walnuts

A little bit goes a long way when it comes to walnuts. Eating just one ounce of these nuts every week can reduce a woman's risk of developing gallstones by 25 percent.

 Variation

Use ½ cup whole grain bread crumbs instead of the bread, and then add the seasonings listed.

Veggie Burgers with Millet and Sweet Potatoes

Serve the burgers in whole wheat pitas with lettuce, chopped tomatoes and *Cucumber Dill Dressing* (page 28) or *Ranch Dressing* (page 29). The consistency of these patties is a bit more crumbly than store-bought frozen patties because we don't use gums or artificial binding ingredients.

Makes about 8, 3-inch burgers.

½ cup millet

1½ cup water

(Or 2 cups cooked millet)

½ unpeeled large sweet potato (about ½ pound)

⅓ bunch parsley (stems OK)

½ medium onion

1 unpeeled carrot

¼ cup pecans

¼ cup sunflower seeds

Heaping ½ teaspoon cumin seeds

Heaping ½ teaspoon fennel seeds

Heaping ½ teaspoon ground coriander

½ teaspoon salt

2 eggs

Several generous grindings of pepper

1. Preheat the oven to 400 degrees and oil a jelly roll pan (or a cookie sheet).

2. Prepare the millet with the water according to the directions in *Hot Millet Cereal* (page 150), omitting the salt.

3. While the millet cooks, cut the sweet potato into ½-inch cubes. Put them on the prepared pan and bake for 25 minutes.

4. While the sweet potato bakes, cut 1 to 2 inches off the bottom of the parsley. Using a food processor, finely chop the parsley, onion and carrot. Add the remaining ingredients to the food processor and pulse to incorporate.

5. When the millet and sweet potato are cooked, add them to the food processor and pulse to incorporate. The mixture should be very well diced but not mushy.

6. Oil the jelly roll pan again. Scoop up the veggie burger mixture using a heaping ⅓-cup measure and drop onto the prepared pan. Flatten and shape each burger into a patty, about 3 inches in diameter and ¾ inch thick.

7. Bake the veggie burgers for about 20 to 25 minutes, or until the burgers are golden brown.

 Love Thy Leftovers

With the other half of the sweet potato, you can make half a batch of *Sweet Potato Fries* (page 21). You can also use it in *Lentil Rice Soup* (page 122).

Quinoa with Feta, Capers and Sun-Dried Tomatoes

Makes about 6 cups.

1 medium onion
1 tablespoon extra virgin olive oil

2 cups chicken or vegetable broth

⅓ cup sun-dried tomatoes

1 cup quinoa

1 medium zucchini

3 tablespoons capers, drained
¼ cup pine nuts
3 to 6 ounces feta cheese
Several generous grindings of pepper

Salt to taste

1. Chop the onion and sauté in the olive oil in a large saucepan over medium heat until it begins to soften, about 5 minutes.

2. Add the broth to the saucepan and bring to a boil over medium-high heat.

3. While the broth is heating:

   a. Chop the sun-dried tomatoes and set aside. (If you are using oil-packed sun-dried tomatoes, shake off the excess oil before using.)

   b. If you are not using prewashed quinoa, wash the quinoa well using a fine mesh strainer. (If the quinoa can fit through your strainer's holes, line it with a coffee filter first.)

4. Once the broth is boiling, add the quinoa and sun-dried tomatoes and cover the pot. Simmer over low heat until the liquid is absorbed, about 20 minutes.

5. While the quinoa cooks, cut the zucchini into bite-sized pieces. When the quinoa is cooked (it is done when the grain becomes transparent and the spiral-like germ separates), add the chopped zucchini. Allow the steam to slightly cook the zucchini for 2 to 3 minutes.

6. Add the capers, pine nuts, feta cheese and pepper and mix to incorporate. Add salt if needed and serve warm, at room temperature or cold.

 Divine Design: Quinoa

The Creator provided many different grains, all with different characteristics. Quinoa has the highest protein content of all grains.

Variations

⊙ Use sliced or chopped olives instead of the capers.

⊙ Use several cups of fresh spinach, torn into bite-sized pieces, instead of the zucchini.

Quesadillas

Makes 2 servings.

2 to 4 ounces Monterey Jack, Colby, mozzarella or other cheese

---

2, 8-inch whole wheat tortillas

OPTIONAL FILLINGS (USE 1 TO 2 TABLESPOONS OF EACH FILLING PER QUESADILLA)
- Finely chopped vegetables (such as bell peppers, onions, avocados, black olives or tomatoes)
- Refried beans from *Refried Bean Wraps* (page 105)
- *Basic Roasted Vegetables* (page 15)
- Chopped *Basic Cooked Chicken* (page 74)
- Shredded spinach leaves

OPTIONAL TOPPINGS (SPOON 1 TO 2 TABLESPOONS OF EACH ON TOP BEFORE SERVING)
- Salsa
- *Guacamole* (page 191)

1. Shred the cheese.

2. Place one of the tortillas in a large frying pan and sprinkle half of the tortilla with half of the shredded cheese and any optional fillings.

3. Fold the tortilla in half and cook over medium-high heat for 2 to 4 minutes per side, or until the cheese is melted and the vegetables have softened slightly. Remove from the pan.

4. Repeat the process with the other tortilla.

5. Cut the quesadillas in half or into quarters and top with any optional toppings before serving.

Divine Design: Cheese

Cheese is one way you can see the divine design for your health. Even when refrigerators did not exist, butter, yogurt and cheese were available as God's natural medication for high blood pressure, osteoporosis, cavities and cholesterol. And choosing organic will help you stay even closer to God's design.

Variations

- Put the optional toppings inside the quesadilla instead of on the top.

- For an "Italian" quesadilla, use crumbled feta or goat cheese instead of the hard cheese and add chopped rehydrated sun-dried tomatoes, a few shredded basil leaves and pine nuts.

Egg Salad

Serve egg salad on a bed of greens or on whole gain bread, or use whole grain crackers to scoop and eat it.

Makes about 3 cups.

6 eggs

1 unpeeled carrot
⅓ bunch parsley (mostly leaves)
¼ medium onion

¼ cup plain yogurt
¼ cup mayonnaise
Heaping ¼ teaspoon salt
Several generous grindings of pepper

OPTIONAL INGREDIENTS
- Finely diced celery
- Finely diced green pepper
- Dijon mustard
- Prepared horseradish
- Pickle relish (or finely diced pickles)
- Finely diced cilantro leaves

1. Fill a medium saucepan with water and bring to a boil. Use enough water to sufficiently cover the eggs.

2. When the water is boiling, gently place the eggs in the saucepan with a slotted spoon.

3. Cook the eggs for 13 minutes. Remove them gently with a slotted spoon. (It is OK if any eggs crack while cooking.)

4. Transfer the eggs to a bowl, run cold water over them for 1 minute, and leave the eggs in the water to cool. As the eggs cool:

   a. Finely chop the carrot, parsley and onion. Place in a medium bowl.

   b. Add the remaining ingredients, including any optional ingredients, to the bowl.

5. When the eggs are cool, crack each one and peel away the shell.

6. Finely chop the eggs and add to the bowl. Mix well to incorporate.

Divine Design: Eggs

Egg yolks contain cholesterol. Did God make a mistake? Not a chance! Not only are the yolks filled with essential vitamins and minerals, but the egg whites contain lecithin—an enzyme that helps your body use cholesterol in a way that helps you, not harms you. The yolks are also rich in choline, an essential nutrient that boosts cardiovascular health and helps the nervous system function.

Variations

- Experiment with different proportions of yogurt and mayonnaise.

- To prepare in a food processor, first pulse the carrot, parsley, onion and any optional vegetables until finely chopped. Then add the other ingredients and process until combined. Add the hard-boiled eggs last and pulse until the egg salad reaches the desired consistency.

Quiche

Makes about 4 servings.

1 medium onion

1 tablespoon extra virgin olive oil

4 cups firmly packed fresh spinach (about 5 ounces)

4 to 8 ounces cheese (such as cheddar or feta)

4 eggs

½ cup milk or rice milk

2 tablespoons whole wheat, whole spelt or oat flour

¼ to ½ teaspoon salt

Several generous grindings of pepper

Heaping ½ teaspoon dried herbs (such as basil, thyme or rosemary)

Store-bought whole grain pie crust, unbaked

1. Preheat the oven to 375 degrees.

2. Chop the onion, coat the bottom of a frying pan with the olive oil, and sauté the onion over medium-high heat.

3. While the onion cooks, wash the spinach and remove the stems. Drain and dry it very well. Chop or tear the spinach into bite-sized strips.

4. When the onion is soft, add the spinach and sauté for about 1 minute, or until slightly wilted. Remove from the heat and set aside.

5. Depending on the type of cheese you are using, shred or crumble the cheese and set aside.

6. In a blender or food processor, combine the next six ingredients (eggs through herbs). Blend until well incorporated.

7. To assemble the quiche:

   a. Sprinkle the cheese in the pie crust.

   b. Spread the spinach mixture over the cheese.

   c. Pour the egg mixture over the cheese and spinach mixture. If the pan is very full, set it on a cookie sheet.

8. Bake the quiche for 30 to 40 minutes, or until the egg mixture is set in the middle.

Variations

- Instead of a store-bought crust, make your own rice crust by mixing 2 cups leftover brown rice, 1 egg and ½ teaspoon salt. Press into an oiled 9-inch pie pan, assemble and bake the quiche according to the directions.

- Omit the crust and bake the quiche in a well-oiled 8 x 8-inch baking pan.

- Add 4 to 6 chopped rehydrated sun-dried tomatoes to the spinach mixture.

- Add a few tablespoons of *Turkey Sausage* (page 86) to the pie pan during step 7.

Chapter 5
Soup, Stew and Chili

Esau sold his birthright to Isaac in exchange for some stew. We don't know if the "red stuff" referred to in Genesis 25 was similar to our *Red Lentil Soup*, but we certainly understand Esau's hankering. Soup, stew and chili are comforting, tasty, easy to prepare and nutritious.

The recipes in this chapter have several things in common. First, they do not have any Love Thy Leftovers tips. Why? Most of these dishes taste better after a day or two, so we recommend just reheating them. Also, most soups freeze well. If you do not want to eat leftovers several days in a row, ladle them into an airtight container and freeze them.

Next, these recipes call for less salt than most people prefer. Please don't misunderstand: God gave us salt to preserve our food and to make it taste better, as long as we use it in moderation. And while the media paints salt/sodium as evil, this God-given ingredient is actually an important nutrient in our diet. We like salt! We've simply chosen to start low in order to cater to people's wide variety of tastes. In other words, it is easier to add more salt than it is to remove it.

As with all our recipes, we encourage you to add enough salt to suit your taste. In most cases, you will be adding less than is found in most commercial and restaurant soups—even if it feels like you are adding a lot. Along the same lines, your broth may vary greatly in flavor and salt content. Accordingly, you will need to adjust the salt in the recipes depending on what broth you use.

Finally, while the ingredients in all of our recipes are flexible, the recipes in this chapter are especially open to creativity. For example, in almost any recipe you can add leftover rice, barley, millet or other cooked grains; add additional vegetables; vary the amount of liquid used (for thicker or thinner dishes); or tweak the amount of spices or other ingredients. You should do plenty of tasting and adjusting before you serve these dishes. This is especially true of our "'Cream' of . . ." soups, which basically feature a vegetable (squash, broccoli, spinach or potatoes), liquid and some seasonings. The lack of firm direction in these recipes is an invitation to experimentation!

Principle 1

Nearly every vegetable, bean, grain, herb and animal that God designed can be used to make soup, stew or chili.

Principle 2

Since you are starting with fresh vegetables and no preservatives or additives, homemade soup is much closer to God's design than boxed or canned soup.

Principle 3

Eating soup for lunch can actually help you avoid food idolatry. Studies have shown that people who eat soup feel more satisfied after they eat, and they therefore eat less later in the day.

Fish Chowder

Makes about 3 quarts.

1 large onion
2 garlic cloves
Extra virgin olive oil

2 unpeeled carrots
2 celery stalks

1 pound unpeeled potatoes
1 small zucchini

2 cups chicken or vegetable broth
2 cups tomato juice (or chicken or vegetable broth)
1, 14-ounce can of chopped tomatoes, undrained (or 2 medium tomatoes, chopped)
Heaping ½ teaspoon fennel seeds
Heaping ½ teaspoon dried tarragon
Dash of cayenne pepper
Heaping ½ teaspoon salt
Several generous grindings of pepper

1 pound skinless tilapia, turbo, cod or other white flaky fish fillet

1. Chop the onions and garlic.

2. Coat the bottom of a stockpot with olive oil (about 2 tablespoons) and sauté the onions and garlic over medium-high heat.

3. While the onions and garlic cook, dice the carrots and celery and add them to the pot.

4. Dice the potatoes and zucchini and add them to the pot.

5. Add the remaining ingredients (except the fish) to the pot. Mix to incorporate and bring to a boil.

6. Reduce the heat and simmer, partially covered, until the potatoes are tender, about 20 to 30 minutes.

7. Wash the fish fillets and cut into 1-inch pieces. Add to the chowder, making sure that the fish is submerged in the liquid. Cook for another 10 to 15 minutes, until the fish flakes easily with a fork. Add additional salt and pepper to taste.

Divine Design: Celery

The Creator made every part of this plant for your enjoyment and benefit. God filled the crunchy stalks with vitamin C, potassium and calcium, while infusing an even higher concentration of these same nutrients into the celery leaves. And don't forget the seeds! They add iron to your soups, stews or casseroles.

Chicken and Rice Soup with Spinach

Makes about 3 quarts.

2 medium onions
Extra virgin olive oil

2 unpeeled carrots
2 celery stalks

5 cups chicken broth
¾ cup brown rice

4 cups firmly packed fresh spinach
(or 5 ounces frozen spinach)
⅓ bunch parsley (mostly leaves)
3 to 4 sprigs of fresh dill

½ to ¾ pound boneless, skinless
chicken breasts

Heaping ½ teaspoon salt
Several generous grindings of pepper

1. Chop the onions.

2. Coat the bottom of a stockpot with olive oil (about 2 tablespoons) and sauté the onions over medium-high heat.

3. Chop the carrots and celery. Add to the pot and cook until soft, about 6 to 8 minutes.

4. Add the broth and rice to the pot, bring to a boil, reduce the heat to low, and cover. Simmer for 45 minutes.

5. Meanwhile, chop the spinach into bite-sized pieces and finely chop the parsley and dill. Set aside.

6. Wash the chicken, chop into bite-sized pieces, and add to the pot once the rice has cooked for 45 minutes.

7. Add the salt and pepper and continue cooking for an additional 15 minutes, until the chicken is no longer pink.

8. Stir in the spinach, parsley and dill. Cook until wilted and heated through. (If you are using frozen spinach, just add it to the pot and cook until thawed and heated.) Add additional salt and pepper to taste.

Divine Design: Spinach

This bitter herb may lead to rich mental health. Snacking on this specially designed ingredient may prevent some signs of aging by improving motor skills and learning capacity.

Variation

Use 1 heaping teaspoon dried parsley and/or ½ teaspoon dried dill in place of the fresh herbs. Add to the pot in step 4.

Lamb Stew

Makes about 2 quarts.

1 large onion
2 garlic cloves
Extra virgin olive oil

1 pound lamb stew meat

3 cups chicken, vegetable or beef broth
½ cup split peas (green or yellow), green or brown lentils, or a combination

3 unpeeled carrots
2 celery stalks

1 unpeeled medium potato
½ to ¾ teaspoon salt
½ teaspoon ground cumin
Several generous grindings of pepper

¼ to ⅓ bunch parsley (mostly leaves; optional)

1. Chop the onion and garlic.

2. Coat the bottom of a stockpot with olive oil (about 2 tablespoons) and sauté the onion and garlic over medium-high heat.

3. Cut the lamb into ¼- to ½-inch pieces, removing any extra fat. Add the lamb to the onion and garlic, and sauté until browned, about 10 minutes.

4. Once the lamb is cooked, add the broth and peas or lentils to the pot.

5. Cut the carrots and celery into small pieces and add to the pot. Allow the stew to simmer over low heat, partially covered, until the peas or lentils, carrots and celery are soft, about 30 minutes.

6. Shred or finely chop the potato and add to the pot. Add the salt, cumin and pepper. Allow the stew to simmer for an additional 30 minutes, or until the stew is thickened by the cooked potato. Add additional salt and pepper to taste.

7. Chop the parsley (if using) and sprinkle it over the stew before serving.

 Divine Design: Lamb

For Passover, God commanded His people to kill and eat a lamb. Just as the Israelites trusted God to protect them from the plague of death (by spreading the lamb's blood on their doorposts), so too can you trust Him to provide you with nutrients to protect you from sickness and disease by following His design for eating, which includes nutrient-rich meats like lamb.

Variation

Experiment with different types of meats, such as boneless skinless chicken breast or beef stew meat.

Lentil Rice Soup

Makes about 2½ quarts.

1 medium onion
1 to 2 garlic cloves
Extra virgin olive oil

1 unpeeled carrot
1 celery stalk

1 tablespoon dried parsley
Heaping ½ teaspoon salt
½ teaspoon dried oregano
½ teaspoon dried marjoram
½ teaspoon dried basil
Heaping ¼ teaspoon dried thyme
Several generous grindings of pepper
4 cups chicken or vegetable broth
½ cup green or brown lentils
¼ cup brown rice

½ unpeeled large sweet potato (about
  ½ pound)

2 kale stalks
1 medium tomato (optional) (or 1 cup canned
  chopped tomatoes, drained)

1. Chop the onion and garlic.

2. Coat the bottom of a stockpot with olive oil (about 2 tablespoons) and sauté the onion and garlic over medium-high heat.

3. While the onion cooks, chop the carrot and celery. Add to the pot and sauté until they begin to soften.

4. Add the herbs (parsley through pepper), broth, lentils and rice. Mix well and continue cooking over medium-high heat.

5. Dice the sweet potato, add it to the pot, and bring to a boil. Once the soup is boiling, turn the heat to low and simmer, partially covered, until the rice and sweet potato are tender, about 1 hour from the time you add the broth.

6. While the soup is simmering, tear the kale into bite-sized pieces and chop the tomato (if using).

7. Add the kale and tomato during the last 10 minutes of cooking. Add additional salt and pepper to taste.

Divine Design: Kale

Do you think of dairy first when you need calcium in your diet? Think again! Kale, a dark green member of the cabbage family, is an excellent source of this wonderful nutrient. One cup of cooked kale has more calcium than four ounces of cottage cheese.

 Love Thy Leftovers

Use the other half of the sweet potato to make *Veggie Burgers with Millet and Sweet Potatoes* (page 109) or half a batch of *Sweet Potato Fries* (page 21).

Split Pea Soup

To make this preparation even quicker, use a food processor to chop the vegetables and potatoes.

Makes about 4 quarts.

3 cups split peas (green or yellow)
8 cups chicken or vegetable broth
1 teaspoon salt

1 large onion
4 garlic cloves
3 celery stalks
2 unpeeled carrots

1 unpeeled medium potato

Heaping ½ teaspoon dried thyme
Heaping ½ teaspoon dried basil
Heaping ½ teaspoon dried oregano
Several generous grindings of pepper

1. In a stockpot combine the peas, broth and salt. Bring to a boil, reduce the heat to low, cover, and simmer for 20 to 30 minutes.

2. Finely chop the onion, garlic, celery and carrots and add to the pot.

3. Finely chop the potato and add to the pot.

4. Add the remaining ingredients and mix to incorporate.

5. Partially cover the pot and allow the soup to simmer over low heat for an additional 45 minutes. Add additional salt and pepper to taste.

Divine Design: Split Peas

Split peas (a cousin of the green pea) are packed with fiber and are an excellent source of molybdenum. God created this trace mineral as a powerful weapon against sulfites and other additives that man has added to food.

Variations

⊙ Use green or brown lentils instead of split peas, or use a combination of split peas and lentils.

⊙ Finely chop ¼ to ⅓ bunch parsley. Use it to top the soup before serving.

⊙ Add up to 2 cups chopped fresh or canned tomatoes during the last 10 minutes of cooking.

Red Lentil Soup

Unlike green or brown lentils that retain their shape, red lentils fall apart during cooking and become creamy.

Makes about 2 quarts.

1 large onion
3 garlic cloves
Extra virgin olive oil

3 unpeeled carrots
2 celery stalks
1 medium tomato (or 1 cup canned chopped tomatoes, drained)

1 cup red lentils
5 cups chicken or vegetable broth
1¼ teaspoons ground cumin
½ teaspoon salt

¼ to ⅓ bunch parsley or cilantro (mostly leaves)
Several generous grindings of pepper

1. Chop the onion and garlic.

2. Coat the bottom of a stockpot with olive oil (about 2 tablespoons) and sauté the onion and garlic over medium-high heat.

3. While the onion and garlic cook, chop the carrots, celery and tomato and add to the pot.

4. Sauté for several minutes, until the vegetables begin to soften.

5. Add the lentils, broth, cumin and salt to the pot, bring to a boil, and simmer over low heat, partially covered. Stir occasionally and cook for about 30 minutes. At this point the lentils will be very soft and will fall apart easily.

6. While the soup cooks, finely chop the parsley. Before serving, add the parsley and pepper. Add additional salt to taste.

Divine Design: Lentils

God offers the lentil as a fabulous source of low-fat protein and fiber. When you eat lentils, you help reduce your cholesterol and provide your body with energy. No wonder Esau was willing to give up his birthright for them.

Vegetable Barley Soup

Makes about 3 quarts.

1 large onion
2 garlic cloves
Extra virgin olive oil

½ cup barley
5 to 6 cups chicken or vegetable broth
  (depending on how thick you like your soup)
Heaping ½ teaspoon salt
2 teaspoons dried basil
2 teaspoons dried parsley
½ teaspoon dried marjoram
½ teaspoon dried thyme
Several generous grindings of pepper

1 pound mixed vegetables, such as:
- Mushrooms
- Carrots
- Celery
- Peppers
- Zucchini
- Shredded spinach
- Asparagus

1. Chop the onion and garlic.

2. Coat the bottom of a stockpot with olive oil (about 2 tablespoons) and sauté the onion and garlic over medium-high heat.

3. When the onion is soft, add the next eight ingredients (barley through pepper) to the pot. Allow the mixture to come to a boil, cover completely, and simmer over low heat for about 30 minutes.

4. While the barley cooks, chop the vegetables.

5. After 30 minutes, add the vegetables (except spinach and mushrooms) to the pot. Simmer, partially covered, for another 20 to 30 minutes. Stir in the spinach and mushrooms during the last few minutes of cooking, and add additional salt and pepper to taste.

 Divine Design: Barley

When harvested, barley contains its hull, which God created to protect it and extend its shelf life. This hull must be removed before it is eaten. In addition to removing this hull, however, many food manufacturers also "pearl" (or polish) the barley and partially steam it to create quick-cooking barley. When possible, use barley that has been hulled but not pearled. It's closer to God's design—and healthier—than pearled barley.

Variations

- For a beef soup, add ½ pound beef stew meat after completing step 2, and brown the meat before continuing to step 3.

- Experiment with different whole grains, such as brown rice.

Chunky Tomato Soup

Makes about 2 quarts.

1 large onion
2 to 3 garlic cloves
Extra virgin olive oil

2 unpeeled carrots
2 celery stalks

2, 28-ounce cans of chopped tomatoes,
  undrained (or 7 cups chopped fresh
  tomatoes plus 2 cups tomato juice)
1 tablespoon dried basil
2 teaspoons dried parsley
½ teaspoon dried marjoram
¼ teaspoon dried thyme
Heaping ½ teaspoon salt
Several generous grindings of pepper

1. Chop the onion and garlic.

2. Coat the bottom of a stockpot with olive oil (about 2 tablespoons) and sauté the onion and garlic over medium-high heat.

3. While the onion and garlic cook, chop the carrots and celery. Add to the pot and simmer over low heat until all the vegetables are very soft, about 15 to 20 minutes.

4. Add the remaining ingredients. Simmer, partially covered, for 20 minutes and add additional salt and pepper to taste.

 Divine Design: Tomatoes

God placed a potent cancer-fighting carotenoid called lycopene in tomatoes to prevent the growth of cancer cells. This awesome addition teams up with beta-carotene, another God-given nutrient, to keep your body healthy.

Variations

⊙ For a less chunky soup, ladle half or all of the soup into a blender and puree. Return to the pot and heat through.

⊙ For a creamier soup, add ½ cup milk or rice milk to the pot during step 4.

⊙ Experiment by adding other vegetables in step 3, such as yellow bell peppers or corn.

Creamy Black Bean and Cilantro Soup

Makes about 2½ quarts.

1 large onion
3 to 4 garlic cloves
Extra virgin olive oil
1 tablespoon cumin seeds

1 small cauliflower
2 cups chicken or vegetable broth

2-inch piece of fresh ginger

2, 15-ounce cans of black beans, undrained

1 bunch cilantro (mostly leaves)

Heaping ½ teaspoon salt
Several generous grindings of pepper

1. Chop the onion and garlic.

2. Coat the bottom of a stockpot with olive oil (about 2 tablespoons) and sauté the onion, garlic and cumin seeds over medium-high heat.

3. Coarsely chop the cauliflower or break it into pieces.

4. Add the cauliflower and broth to the pot. Bring the broth to a boil. Reduce the heat to medium-low and simmer, partially covered, until the cauliflower is very soft, about 20 to 30 minutes.

5. While the cauliflower cooks, peel the ginger, grate or chop it, and add it to the pot.

6. Add the beans (undrained) to the pot.

7. When the cauliflower is soft, transfer the soup and the cilantro (in several batches) to a food processor or blender. Puree until smooth.

8. Return the soup to the pot, add the salt and pepper, and simmer until heated through. Add additional salt and pepper to taste.

Divine Design: Cilantro

The Creator has given you a simple and delicious cure for mercury and lead poisoning: cilantro. If you think you have been affected by these substances, a combination of seeking your doctor's wisdom and recognizing God's wisdom in creating these healthy greens can bring you back to health.

Variation

Experiment with different garnishes, such as finely diced green pepper, chopped tomatoes or salsa.

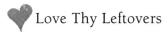

Love Thy Leftovers

If you bought more fresh ginger than needed for the soup, wrap the remaining ginger (unpeeled) in foil and place in the freezer. When you are ready to use ginger again, simply remove from the freezer, peel and grate.

"Cream" of Squash Soup

While the name might have "cream" in it, this soup is very light and can be made dairy free. Pureed squash gives this soup plenty of creaminess and taste. Be brave with this recipe: it does not provide exact measurements because squash sizes vary greatly. Just add your ingredients slowly, tasting as you go.

1 winter squash (such as butternut, acorn, pumpkin or delicata, or a combination)

Milk, rice milk or broth
Several dashes of salt
Several generous grindings of pepper

1. Wash the squash and cut it in half. Use your biggest, sharpest knife and be careful. Scoop out the seeds and as much of the stringy stuff as you can. (If you want to eat the seeds, see the variation to *Cajun-Spiced Pumpkin Seeds*, page 200.)

2. Cut the squash halves into large pieces. Using a rice cooker/ steamer or a stovetop steamer, steam the squash for about 30 minutes, or until the flesh is very soft. Reserve the steaming liquid.

3. Cool the squash slightly and scoop the flesh into a blender or food processor. Add some of the steaming liquid and puree until the squash is smooth.

4. Transfer the squash to a pot and heat on medium-low. Stir in additional cooking liquid or milk, up to ¼ cup at a time, until you reach the desired consistency.

5. Add salt and pepper to taste.

 Variations

- If you don't have a steamer, prepare the squash according to steps 1 and 2, brush with oil, and bake, flesh side down, in a 400 degree oven for 20 to 30 minutes, or until tender. Or simply add an inch of water to a large pot and steam the squash over medium-high heat until tender.

- Experiment by adding a roasted or sautéed onion, sweet potato, carrot and/or yellow or orange bell pepper to the blender in step 3.

- Experiment by adding different ingredients to the steamer, such as an apple or a pear.

- Experiment by adding different spices to the pot in step 5, such as ground cinnamon, nutmeg, ginger or curry.

"Cream" of Spinach Soup

Makes 2 to 3 cups.

1 bunch spinach

1 medium onion

Milk, rice milk or broth
Several dashes of salt
Several generous grindings of pepper

1. Wash the spinach, slice off the very bottom (root) of any stems, and drain in a colander. It does not need to be dry.

2. Cut the onion into large chunks.

3. Using a rice cooker/steamer or a stovetop steamer, steam the spinach and onion until the spinach is wilted and the onion is soft, about 20 minutes. Reserve the steaming liquid.

4. In a food processor or blender, puree the spinach and onion until smooth.

5. Transfer the spinach mixture into a medium saucepan and heat over low. If necessary, add some of the steaming liquid or milk to obtain the desired consistency and creaminess. You will not need very much.

6. Add salt and pepper to taste.

 Variations

- Add 1 to 2 teaspoons olive oil or butter in step 6.

- Instead of steaming the spinach and onion, sauté them in a pan: Slice or chop the onion and sauté with 1 tablespoon olive oil over medium-high heat until soft, about 8 minutes. Add the spinach and sauté until wilted, about 5 minutes. Proceed with step 4.

"Cream" of Broccoli Soup

Makes 4 to 6 cups.

1 bunch broccoli (about 1½ pounds)

1 medium onion

Milk, rice milk or broth
Several dashes of salt
Several generous grindings of pepper

1 to 2 cups shredded cheddar cheese

1. Cut off the bottom inch of the broccoli stems and discard.

2. Cut the broccoli (florets and stems) and the onion into large chunks.

3. Using a rice cooker/steamer or a stovetop steamer, steam the broccoli and onion for about 25 to 35 minutes, or until they are very soft. Reserve the steaming liquid.

4. Puree the broccoli and onion in a blender until smooth, adding some of the steaming liquid to the food processor as needed.

5. Transfer the puree into a medium saucepan and heat over low heat. Add milk to obtain the desired consistency and creaminess, and add salt and pepper to taste.

6. Ladle into bowls and sprinkle with the shredded cheddar cheese before serving.

 Divine Design: Broccoli

When choosing this fantastic vegetable, grab the darker—practically purple—stalks. The dark color is God's marker that it's packed with disease-fighting beta-carotene.

Variations

⊙ Substitute 1 to 2 bunches of asparagus for the broccoli.

⊙ Experiment with different cheeses, such as feta or cream cheese.

⊙ Substitute chicken or vegetable broth for some or all of the milk.

"Cream" of Potato Soup

Makes about 2½ quarts.

4 unpeeled medium potatoes (any variety, including sweet potatoes)

1 medium onion

2 to 4 garlic cloves

Milk, rice milk or broth

Heaping ½ teaspoon salt

2 teaspoons dried dill

Several generous grindings of pepper

1 to 2 cups shredded cheddar cheese

1. Cut the potatoes and onion into 1-inch chunks.

2. Put the potatoes, onion and whole garlic cloves in a medium saucepan and cover with water.

3. Bring the water to a boil and cook until the potatoes are tender and can be easily pierced with a fork, about 15 to 20 minutes.

4. When the potatoes are tender, reserve several cups of the liquid. Then drain the potato mixture in a colander.

5. Puree about 1 cup of the potato mixture, including all the cooked garlic cloves, in a blender or food processor. Add the reserved potato water as needed.

6. Pour the potato puree back into the pot with the remaining potatoes and onions. Add the reserved liquid or milk as needed to obtain the desired consistency and creaminess. Use a potato masher to break up any potato or onion pieces (if desired).

7. Add the salt, dill and pepper. Mix to incorporate and add additional salt and pepper to taste.

8. Ladle into bowls and sprinkle with the shredded cheddar cheese before serving.

Divine Design: Potatoes

Did you know that God filled potatoes with as much potassium as bananas? Since potassium helps stabilize your body's salt levels, it has a calming effect on blood pressure. Potatoes are also rich in vitamin C.

Variations

- For a less chunky soup, puree more than 1 cup of the potato mixture and add additional liquid.

- Use baked potatoes instead of boiled potatoes. Sauté the onion and garlic in olive oil on the stovetop before adding the baked potatoes. Add milk or broth and puree as indicated.

- Substitute 1 or 2 leeks for the onion.

- Tear ½ bunch kale into bite-sized pieces and add to the pot during the last 5 minutes of boiling.

- Sprinkle the soup with chopped chives or fresh thyme before serving.

Gazpacho

As you chop the vegetables for this cold soup in your food processor, puree them as finely or coarsely as you like.

Makes about 2½ quarts.

1 bell pepper (any color)

1 large red onion
3 green onions (white and some green)

1 unpeeled cucumber
3 medium tomatoes (or 1½ pints grape or cherry tomatoes)

⅓ bunch parsley (mostly leaves)
2 large garlic cloves
Juice of 3 limes (about 6 tablespoons)
2 tablespoons extra virgin olive oil
2 tablespoons red or white wine vinegar
Several generous grindings of pepper
½ to 1 teaspoon salt

2 cups tomato or vegetable juice

1. Quarter and seed the pepper and add it to the food processor. Pulse until it is finely chopped and transfer to a large mixing bowl.

2. Coarsely chop the red onion and green onions. Add to the food processor and pulse until they are finely chopped. Transfer to the bowl.

3. Repeat step 2 with the cucumber and again with the tomatoes.

4. Add the next seven ingredients (parsley through salt) to the food processor and process until smooth. Transfer to the bowl.

5. Add the juice to the bowl and mix well to incorporate.

6. Refrigerate for at least 1 hour and serve chilled.

Divine Design: Onions

Unlike stoplights, the colors yellow and red don't mean "slow down" and "stop" when it comes to onions. In fact, these colors mean "go!" Yellow and red onions have the highest content of flavonoids—powerful antioxidants that help prevent disease.

Variations

⊙ Add a seeded jalapeño or Anaheim chile during step 4.

⊙ Substitute a carrot for the bell pepper.

⊙ Experiment with using cilantro instead of parsley.

⊙ Use the juice of 1½ lemons instead of the limes.

Meat Chili

Makes about 4½ quarts.

1 large onion
3 garlic cloves
Extra virgin olive oil

1 to 1½ pounds lean ground beef or turkey (or
  a combination)

1 green bell pepper

1 tablespoon dried parsley
1 teaspoon dried oregano
2 heaping tablespoons chili powder
1 tablespoon cumin seeds
1 heaping teaspoon salt
Several generous grindings of pepper
1, 15-ounce can of kidney beans, undrained
1, 15-ounce can of white beans, undrained
1, 28-ounce can of chopped tomatoes,
  undrained
1, 6-ounce can of tomato paste
Up to 1 cup tomato juice or chicken,
  vegetable or beef broth (optional)

1. Chop the onion and garlic.

2. Coat the bottom of a stockpot with olive oil (about 2 tablespoons) and sauté the onion and garlic over medium-high heat until the onion begins to soften, about 5 minutes.

3. Add the ground meat and cook until mostly browned, stirring frequently to break up the meat pieces.

4. While the meat cooks, chop the pepper and add it to the pot. Cook for an additional 5 minutes, until the pepper begins to soften.

5. Add the remaining ingredients, stir well, and bring to a boil. (For a thicker chili, omit the optional tomato juice or broth.)

6. Reduce the heat to low and simmer, partially covered, for 30 minutes, stirring occasionally. (To allow the flavors to develop more fully, cook for 1 hour or more instead of 30 minutes.) Add additional salt and pepper to taste.

 Divine Design: Beef

The leaner the cut, the greater the benefit. God made lean beef a good source of vitamins B6 and B12, which fight heart disease, osteoporosis and colon cancer. The leanest beef is found on the back leg bone, which is where eye of round, top round and bottom round come from.

Variations

⊙ If you do not have cumin seeds, use 2 teaspoons ground cumin.

⊙ Experiment with different beans, such as garbanzo or pinto beans.

⊙ Use beef stew meat instead of ground meat.

⊙ Replace half of the meat with cooked *Turkey Sausage* (page 86) in step 5.

Black Bean Chili

Makes about 2 quarts.

1 large onion
Extra virgin olive oil

1 unpeeled carrot

2 medium tomatoes (or 1, 14-ounce can of chopped tomatoes, drained)

2, 15-ounce cans of black beans, undrained
1 cup frozen corn
¼ cup orange juice or the juice of ½ lemon or 1 lime (about 2 tablespoons)
2 teaspoons dried oregano
1 tablespoon ground cumin
1 teaspoon ground coriander
Heaping ½ teaspoon salt
Heaping ½ teaspoon chili powder
Heaping ¼ teaspoon paprika
Several generous grindings of pepper

Chopped fresh cilantro and/or avocado (optional)

1. Chop the onion.

2. Coat the bottom of a stockpot with olive oil (about 2 tablespoons) and sauté the onion over medium-high heat.

3. While the onion cooks:

   a. Dice the carrot and add it to the onion mixture. Continue cooking until the onion is soft.

   b. Dice the tomatoes.

4. When the onion is soft, add the tomatoes and the remaining ingredients (except cilantro and avocado) to the pot. Mix to incorporate and allow the chili to simmer over low heat, partially covered, for about 10 to 15 minutes. Add additional salt and pepper to taste.

5. Top with the cilantro and/or avocado (if using) before serving.

Divine Design: Black Beans

Just one cup of black beans contains 20 percent of the daily value of iron. And best of all? The Creator made them low in calories and practically fat free.

 Variations

- Add *Basic Cooked Rice* (page 39) or chopped *Basic Cooked Chicken* (page 74) to the chili.
- Dice half of a red bell pepper and add during step 3.

Vegetable Chili

Makes about 2½ quarts.

1 large onion

2 garlic cloves

1 to 2 cups mixed, chopped vegetables, such as:

- 1 unpeeled carrot
- 1 bell pepper (any color)
- 1 small zucchini

Extra virgin olive oil

2, 15-ounce cans of beans (such as kidney, pinto, white, garbanzo), undrained

1, 28-ounce can of chopped tomatoes, undrained

1, 6-ounce can of tomato paste

½ cup frozen corn

1½ teaspoons dried oregano

1 heaping teaspoon ground cumin

1 heaping teaspoon chili powder

1 heaping teaspoon dried basil

Heaping ½ teaspoon salt

Several generous grindings of pepper

1. Chop the onion, garlic and any other vegetables you are using.

2. Coat the bottom of a stockpot with olive oil (about 2 tablespoons) and sauté the onion and garlic over medium-high heat until they begin to soften, about 5 minutes.

3. Add the other vegetables and sauté for about 5 minutes.

4. Add the remaining ingredients to the pot, mix to incorporate, and bring to a boil.

5. Simmer over low heat, partially covered, until the vegetables are soft, about 20 minutes. Add additional salt and pepper to taste.

 Variations

- Experiment with different garnishes, such as chopped avocados, olives or onions.
- Serve over *Basic Cooked Rice* (page 39), whole grain pasta or *Spaghetti Squash* (page 20).

Chapter 6
Breakfast

"Come and have breakfast." While few Americans follow Jesus' example of serving fish for breakfast (except when we have bagels and lox), it is good to know that the risen Messiah encouraged His disciples to partake in this meal (according to the Apostle John's account of the story).

By now you have probably heard why it is important to start the day by "breaking the fast" of the past twelve hours or so: refueling feeds your brain, helps you function at work, reduces your chances of overeating at lunch and gives you energy for the whole day. Just as you are designed to sleep at night, you are also designed to nourish your body when you rise.

So what type of breakfast are we suggesting? We recommend whole grains and fruit (since complex carbohydrates are classic body fuel), as well as some component of protein. The recipes in this chapter are designed to provide these elements to give you the good start you need.

Most of these recipes admittedly take more time than grabbing a store-bought muffin or donut on the way to work. But try this test: eat only Creator-based breakfasts for one week and see how your energy level increases.

If you are looking for speed and simplicity, make *Hot Oat Cereal* using oat bran. Or carve out an hour after work and make *Fruit and Nut Granola* or *Coconut Almond Granola*. They are easy to prepare, make a ton (you will have breakfast for over a week) and taste delicious. Over the weekend try the *Spinach "Soufflé"* or the *Multigrain Pancakes*. Depending on your family size, these weekend treats make great leftovers that you can eat during the week for breakfast, lunch or a hearty snack.

Many of our breakfast recipes contain ranges for the sweetener. If you like foods that are not too sweet or want to reduce your sugar intake, use the low end of the range; if you prefer sweeter breakfast foods and desserts, use the larger amount.

Principle 1

It is easy to get in a rut, eating the same breakfast every day. Make the effort to include in your breakfasts a variety of the fruits, grains, nuts and even vegetables that God has provided.

Principle 2

It is easier to buy store-bought pancake mix, muffin mix, cereals and breads, but you will feel better if you make your own. Most of these recipes freeze well, so make double or triple batches and freeze the leftovers.

Principle 3

While fruit and whole grains are the backbone of our breakfast recipes, be sure to include healthy fats and proteins (such as whole milk yogurt, cheese, nut butter or nuts) in your breakfast. This will help you feel full for longer and give you sustained energy throughout the morning.

Banana Bread

Make sure your bananas show brown ripening freckles for this recipe. If they are not ripe enough, you will lose some flavor.

Makes 1 loaf.

DRY INGREDIENTS
½ cup walnuts
1½ cups whole wheat or whole spelt flour
1 teaspoon baking soda
½ teaspoon salt

WET INGREDIENTS
3 large or 4 small ripe bananas
¼ cup extra virgin olive oil
¼ to ⅓ cup honey or maple syrup
1 egg
¼ cup plain yogurt or kefir

1. Preheat the oven to 350 degrees. Oil a standard loaf pan.

2. Chop the walnuts and combine with the remaining dry ingredients in a medium bowl.

3. In a large bowl mash the bananas with a fork or a potato masher. It is OK if they are lumpy—the lumps will make nice little chunks in the bread.

4. Add the remaining wet ingredients to the bananas and combine well.

5. Add the dry ingredients to the banana mixture. Mix enough to moisten.

6. Pour the batter into the loaf pan. Bake until a toothpick inserted into the center of the bread comes out clean, about 45 to 55 minutes. Cool slightly before slicing.

 Divine Design: Bananas

God designed bananas—filled with potassium—to protect you from strokes and heart attacks. They are also a natural antacid and are now being used to aid ulcer treatment.

Variations

- Add up to 2 tablespoons oat bran or flax meal to the dry ingredients.

- For banana muffins, fill 12 lined muffin tins with batter and bake at 350 degrees for 23 to 26 minutes.

- For zucchini bread, substitute 2 shredded small zucchini for the bananas, use ½ to ⅔ cup sweetener, and add 1 teaspoon cinnamon, a heaping ¼ teaspoon nutmeg and 1 teaspoon vanilla.

- For a dessert, add ⅔ cup semisweet chocolate chips to the dry ingredients and use ½ cup sweetener.

- Substitute up to ½ cup oat flour for the whole wheat or whole spelt flour.

Love Thy Leftovers

- Spread leftover banana bread with peanut butter and serve for lunch.

- Refrigerate any extra bread after a day or two.

Ezekiel Bread

Ezekiel bread is often used as a generic term to describe bread made with wheat, barley, beans, lentils, millet and spelt. Its taste is worth the effort, especially with a little butter on it.

Makes 2 loaves.

2 envelopes yeast
2 teaspoons honey
Water

2½ cups whole wheat flour
2½ cups whole spelt flour
2 cups barley flour
1 cup garbanzo bean or other bean flour
1 heaping tablespoon salt

½ cup millet
½ cup green or brown lentils
½ cup extra virgin olive oil
½ cup honey
Water

Whole wheat or whole spelt flour for kneading

1. In a glass measuring cup, combine the yeast, 2 teaspoons honey and ½ cup warm water. Mix to incorporate and allow the mixture to stand for about 10 minutes. During this time, the mixture will grow. Meanwhile:

   a. Add the flours and salt to a large bowl. Mix to incorporate.

   b. In a blender combine the millet, lentils, olive oil, ½ cup honey and ½ cup water. Blend for about 30 seconds. Add 2 additional cups of water and blend again briefly to combine.

2. Pour the lentil mixture and yeast mixture into the flour mixture. Using a wooden spoon, mix until dough is formed.

3. Sprinkle additional flour on a flat surface or clean countertop. Put the dough on the floured surface and knead it for about 5 to 10 minutes. You may need additional flour if the dough is too gooey. During this time, the dough will come together into a smooth, elastic ball.

4. To prevent sticking, rub olive oil on the dough and put it back into the large bowl. Cover the bowl with a clean dishtowel and put the bowl in an unheated oven or other warm, dry place. Allow the dough to rise for 1½ hours or more—it should almost double in size.

5. Remove the dough from the oven and punch it down. Knead it again for several minutes, using additional flour as needed.

6. Split the dough in half and shape into two loaves. Place each loaf into a well-oiled loaf pan and allow them to rise again for 1½ hours or more—they should almost double in size.

7. Bake at 350 degrees for about 40 minutes.

Divine Design: Ezekiel Bread

This bread comes straight from the book of Ezekiel. In verse 4:9 God instructs Ezekiel to make a special type of bread—one that will sustain him for over a year. It includes hearty ingredients such as wheat, barley, beans, lentils, millet and spelt, which are all high in protein, vitamins and minerals.

Variations

⊚ Use 1 can of cooked lentils (rinsed and drained) instead of the raw lentils.

⊚ Use 1 can of garbanzo beans (rinsed and drained) instead of the garbanzo bean flour, and increase the whole wheat flour to 3 cups and the whole spelt flour to 3 cups.

Love Thy Leftovers

⊚ Use leftover Ezekiel bread to make French toast.

⊚ Refrigerate or freeze any extra bread after a day or two.

Blueberry Oat Bran Muffins

Makes about 12 muffins.

DRY INGREDIENTS

1 cup whole wheat or whole spelt flour

¾ cup oat bran

¾ teaspoon baking powder

¼ teaspoon baking soda

¼ teaspoon salt

WET INGREDIENTS

¼ cup extra virgin olive oil

¼ cup honey or maple syrup

¾ cup plain yogurt or kefir

1 egg

2 teaspoons blackstrap molasses (optional)

FRUIT

1¼ to 1½ cups blueberries (fresh or frozen)

1. Preheat the oven to 350 degrees. Oil a muffin tin or line it with paper liners.

2. Combine the dry ingredients in a large bowl.

3. In a glass measuring cup, combine the wet ingredients and mix well to incorporate.

4. Add the wet ingredients to the dry ingredients and mix enough to moisten. Gently add the blueberries and stir to combine.

5. Using a ¼-cup measure to scoop, divide the batter into the muffin cups. Bake until a toothpick inserted into several of the muffins comes out clean, about 20 to 22 minutes.

Divine Design: Blueberries

While fresh blueberries—straight from the Creator—are the healthiest, they are only in season during the middle of the summer. But you can enjoy them year-round, since the freezing process captures the majority of blueberries' nutrients.

 Variations

⊛ Experiment with other berries, such as strawberries or mixed berries.

⊛ Substitute up to ½ cup oat flour for the whole wheat or whole spelt flour.

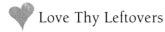 Love Thy Leftovers

These muffins freeze well—just pop them into a freezer bag or other airtight storage container.

Morning Glory Muffins

Makes 12 large muffins.

DRY INGREDIENTS

¾ cup walnuts

2 cups whole wheat or whole spelt flour

Heaping ¼ teaspoon salt

1 teaspoon baking soda

1 teaspoon baking powder

1 tablespoon cinnamon

¾ cup raisins

¼ cup dried unsweetened coconut

WET INGREDIENTS

¾ cup *Applesauce* (page 181) or store-bought applesauce

¼ cup extra virgin olive oil

¼ to ⅓ cup maple syrup

1 egg

2 teaspoons vanilla

INGREDIENTS TO SHRED

2 unpeeled carrots

1 unpeeled apple

1. Preheat the oven to 350 degrees. Oil a muffin tin or line it with paper liners.

2. Chop the walnuts and combine with the other dry ingredients in a large bowl.

3. Combine the wet ingredients in a glass measuring cup and mix well to incorporate.

4. Shred the carrots and apple. Add them to the dry mixture and stir to incorporate.

5. Pour the wet ingredients into the flour mixture and combine well. (The batter will be very thick.)

6. Using a ¼-cup measure to scoop, divide the batter into the muffin cups. The batter will probably reach the top of the cups. Bake until a toothpick inserted into several of the muffins comes out clean and the muffins begin to brown slightly, 25 to 30 minutes.

 Variations

- For morning glory bread, pour the batter into an oiled loaf pan and bake at 350 degrees for 55 to 60 minutes. Allow the bread to cool before slicing.

- Substitute up to 1 cup oat flour for the whole wheat or whole spelt flour.

 Love Thy Leftovers

These muffins freeze well—just pop them into a freezer bag or other storage container.

Fruit and Nut Granola

We think this recipe tastes the best when we use a wide variety of ingredients.

Makes about 9 cups.

⅓ cup extra virgin olive oil

⅓ cup water

⅓ to ½ cup maple syrup or honey

2 teaspoons cinnamon

2 teaspoons vanilla

½ teaspoon salt

3 cups rolled oats

3 cups flakes (any combination of oat, barley, rye and quinoa)

1 cup nuts (any combination of walnuts, almonds, cashews and pecans)

½ cup large seeds (any combination of pumpkin and sunflower)

½ cup small seeds (any combination of flax and sesame)

½ cup any combination of oat bran, wheat bran, ground flax seeds or wheat germ (optional)

1 to 1¼ cups dried fruit (any combination of raisins, currants, apricots, blueberries, dates, etc.)

1. Preheat the oven to 350 degrees.

2. Combine the first six ingredients (olive oil through salt) in a liquid measuring cup. Mix to incorporate.

3. Add the rolled oats and any other flakes to a very large bowl. Pour in the oil mixture and mix to incorporate.

4. Coarsely chop the nuts and add them to the oat mixture.

5. Add the next three ingredients (seeds through bran) and mix to incorporate.

6. Spread the oat mixture onto a large jelly roll pan, using a rubber spatula to make sure it is even. (If your jelly roll pan is small, consider using two pans.)

7. Bake for 35 to 40 minutes, stirring every 15 minutes. The granola is done when it is lightly toasted.

8. While the granola is baking, chop any large dried fruit, such as apricots or dates. Once the granola has cooled, mix in all the dried fruit.

Divine Design: Walnuts and Flax Seeds

Both walnuts and flax seeds are plant sources of omega-3 fatty acids, which God created to improve your cardiovascular system. These essential fatty acids are essential to eat, since your body can't produce them on its own.

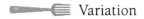 Variation

For peanut butter granola, use ⅔ cup peanut butter instead of the water and increase the salt to a heaping ¼ teaspoon.

 Love Thy Leftovers

If you do not plan to eat all of your granola within 2 weeks, freeze some of it in a plastic container or freezer bag.

Coconut Almond Granola

Makes about 9 cups.

DRY INGREDIENTS

1½ cups almonds

4½ cups rolled oats

1½ cups shredded unsweetened coconut

1½ cups oat bran

½ teaspoon salt

1 teaspoon cinnamon (optional)

WET INGREDIENTS

3 ripe bananas

⅓ cup extra virgin olive oil

⅓ to ½ cup maple syrup or honey

1 teaspoon vanilla

1. Preheat the oven to 350 degrees.

2. Coarsely chop the almonds and combine with the other dry ingredients in a large bowl.

3. Add the wet ingredients to a food processor or blender and process until creamy.

4. Pour the wet ingredients over the dry ingredients and mix to incorporate.

5. Spread the oat mixture onto a large jelly roll pan, using a rubber spatula to make sure it is even. (If your jelly roll pan is small, consider using two pans.)

6. Bake for 45 minutes, stirring every 15 minutes to break up the clumps. The granola is done when it turns golden brown.

7. If the granola is still moist after 45 minutes, turn off the oven and leave the pan in the oven (with the door open) to dry out the granola.

Divine Design: Coconuts

Your body relies on certain acids to help it perform. Coconuts—created by God—are filled with lauric acid (which helps prevent viral or bacterial infections) and fatty acids (which boost energy).

 ## Variations

⊙ Instead of serving granola with milk on it, mix it with plain yogurt (and a bit of honey or all-fruit spread to sweeten it) and top it with fresh or frozen berries or a sliced banana.

⊙ Substitute walnuts or pecans for the almonds.

 ## Love Thy Leftovers

⊙ If you do not plan to eat all of your granola within 2 weeks, freeze some in a plastic container or freezer bag.

⊙ Use leftover granola to make *Granola Bars* (page 196)

Muesli

Make muesli the night before to allow the fruit to rehydrate and become plump and the oats to become creamy.

Makes 2 servings.

⅓ cup walnuts

4 dried apricots

4 dried plums (prunes)

1 tablespoon raisins

⅔ cup rolled oats

1 cup milk or rice milk

⅔ cup plain yogurt

Up to 2 tablespoons honey or maple syrup (optional)

2 tablespoons oat bran or flax seed meal

Several dashes of salt

1. Coarsely chop the walnuts, apricots and dried plums.

2. Combine the walnuts and dried fruit with the remaining ingredients in a bowl or plastic container. Mix well to incorporate.

3. Cover and refrigerate for at least 2 hours or overnight. If desired, add additional milk before serving.

 Divine Design: Dried Plums

Prunes—which are now officially called "dried plums"—are a fantastic source of antioxidants. High in fiber and vitamin A, these smart fruits were created by God to combat cancer, Alzheimer's disease, arthritis and more.

Variations

⊚ Use different dried fruit, such as dates, figs or cherries.

⊚ Experiment with different additions such as cinnamon and coconut.

⊚ Substitute *Applesauce* (page 181) for some or all of the yogurt.

Hot Oat Cereal

For all of our recipes, make sure to use regular oats, not quick cooking.

Makes 1 cup.

CEREAL
½ cup rolled oats
1 cup water, milk or rice milk
Several dashes of salt

TOPPING OPTIONS
⊕ Milk or rice milk
⊕ Honey or maple syrup
⊕ Cinnamon
⊕ Chopped nuts (such as almonds, walnuts, pecans)
⊕ Fresh fruit (such as blueberries, sliced bananas, chopped pears, apples)
⊕ Dried fruit (such as raisins or chopped dates, apricots, figs)
⊕ Seeds (such as pumpkin, flax, sesame)
⊕ Butter

1. In a small saucepan combine the oats, water and salt and bring to a boil over medium-high heat.
2. Cover and reduce the heat to low; cock the lid slightly to let steam escape. Cook for 10 to 15 minutes.
3. Once the cereal is cooked, spoon it into a bowl and add your choice of toppings, for example, rice milk, chopped walnuts, sliced bananas and raisins.

Divine Design: Flax Seeds

Would you believe God created a fat that could help prevent heart attacks and strokes? Believe it! These fats are called omega-3 fatty acids and God placed them in flax seeds to help prevent blood clots from forming.

Variations

⊕ For a crunchier and nuttier cereal, use steel cut oats instead of rolled oats:

—Combine ½ cup oats, 1½ cups water and several dashes of salt in a saucepan.

—Bring the oats and water to a boil over medium-high heat.

—Cover and reduce the heat to low; cock the lid slightly to let steam escape. Cook for 25 to 35 minutes.

⊕ For a quick-cooking cereal similar to Cream of Wheat, use oat bran instead of rolled oats:

—Combine ⅓ cup oat bran, ⅔ cup water and several dashes of salt in a saucepan.

—Cook over medium-low heat until the oat bran has completely absorbed the water, about 3 to 5 minutes.

Hot Millet Cereal

With its nutty flavor, millet lends itself to combinations with fruit, nuts and milk. When you choose your saucepan for cooking the millet, keep in mind that this grain expands to over four times its size when it is cooked.

Makes 2 cups.

CEREAL

½ cup millet

1½ cups water

Several dashes of salt

Milk or rice milk (optional)

TOPPING OPTIONS

- Honey or maple syrup
- Cinnamon
- Chopped nuts (such as almonds, walnuts, pecans)
- Fresh fruit (such as blueberries, sliced bananas, chopped pears, apples)
- Dried fruit (such as raisins or chopped dates, apricots, figs)
- Seeds (such as pumpkin, flax, sesame)
- Butter

1. In a small saucepan combine the millet, water and salt. Bring to a boil over medium-high heat. Cover and reduce the heat to low.

2. Simmer for 25 minutes and turn off the flame. Without opening the lid, let the pot sit for another 5 to 10 minutes to let the millet grains fully absorb the water.

3. Spoon the millet into a bowl and drizzle with milk (if using), so the cereal is moist but not soupy.

4. Add your choice of toppings, for example, cinnamon, chopped pecans and fresh blueberries.

 Divine Design: Millet

God made millet easy to digest and gluten free, so it's good for folks who are sensitive to gluten-filled grains, such as wheat.

 Variation

Instead of millet, prepare *Basic Cooked Rice* (page 39), using water, not broth. Serve it for breakfast using the toppings listed above.

Love Thy Leftovers

Double or triple the recipe for millet so you can make *Millet Casserole* (page 49), *Millet Pilaf* (page 50) or *Veggie Burgers with Millet and Sweet Potatoes* (page 109).

Creamy Brown Rice Cereal

Similar to *Hot Oat Cereal*'s oat bran variation, this breakfast idea is fast, tasty and nutty, with a Cream of Wheat consistency.

Makes about ½ cup.

2 cups water, milk or rice milk
½ cup brown rice
Several dashes of salt

TOPPING OPTIONS
⊚ Honey or maple syrup
⊚ Cinnamon
⊚ Chopped nuts (such as almonds, walnuts, pecans)
⊚ Fresh fruit (such as blueberries, sliced bananas, chopped pears, apples)
⊚ Dried fruit (such as raisins or chopped dates, apricots, figs)
⊚ Seeds (such as pumpkin, flax, sesame)
⊚ Butter

1. In a small saucepan bring the water to a boil over medium-high heat.

2. Grind the rice in a blender until it is floury; the last remaining pieces should be no bigger than coarse salt.

3. Add the ground rice and salt to the saucepan and reduce the heat to medium-low.

4. Cook the rice, stirring frequently to break up the lumps, until it has completely absorbed the liquid, the cereal is bubbly, and there are no longer any crunchy pieces, about 5 to 10 minutes. (The more servings you make, the longer it will take to cook.) The cereal will look similar to Cream of Wheat hot cereal.

5. Once the cereal is cooked, spoon it into a bowl and add your choice of toppings.

 Divine Design: Rice

Nutrient-packed brown rice, in its God-given form, can take almost an hour to cook. Store-bought "quick-cooking" rice solves this problem, but the processing reduces its nutrients. Grinding your own brown rice in the blender keeps all the nutrients of the whole grain, while slashing the cooking time.

Variation

Grind other whole grains, such as millet, barley or oats, instead of the rice.

Basic Scrambled Eggs

Makes 1 serving.

1 to 2 teaspoons extra virgin olive oil

1 or 2 eggs

Several dashes of salt
Several generous grindings of pepper

1. Heat the olive oil in a frying pan over medium-high heat.

2. Crack the eggs into a small bowl and beat slightly with a wire whisk or fork

3. When the oil is hot, add the eggs to the frying pan and scramble using a wooden spoon until just set. Season with salt and pepper.

Divine Design: Eggs

The Creator packed eggs with a large dose of "brain food" called choline, which contributes to healthy brain cell structure and function. It is also a key player in the nervous system, helping transmit messages from the nerves to the muscles.

Variations

⊙ Sprinkle grated cheese into the scrambled eggs while cooking.

⊙ Add salsa to the scrambled eggs while cooking and serve in a whole wheat tortilla. Top with *Guacamole* (page 191).

⊙ In the olive oil, sauté chopped onions, bell peppers, asparagus, spinach, broccoli or any other chopped raw vegetables before adding the eggs. For crispier vegetables, add vegetables to the scrambled eggs without sautéing them first.

⊙ Add diced leftover *Basic Roasted Vegetables* (page 15) to the cooked eggs and heat through before serving.

Spinach "Soufflé"

We use the term *soufflé* loosely here, since this dish is much easier—and more foolproof—than a traditional soufflé. This recipe reheats nicely, so you can prepare it a day ahead if you are expecting company or if you need to bring a dish to a brunch.

Makes about 12, 3 x 4-inch pieces.

FOOD PROCESSOR INGREDIENTS

8 cups firmly packed fresh spinach (or 1, 10-ounce package of fresh or frozen chopped spinach)

2 medium zucchini

1 large onion

OTHER INGREDIENTS

½ cup grated Parmesan cheese

Heaping 1 tablespoon dried parsley

Heaping 1 teaspoon dried oregano

Heaping 1 teaspoon dried basil

¼ cup extra virgin olive oil

6 eggs

Heaping ½ teaspoon salt

Several generous grindings of pepper

1. Preheat the oven to 350 degrees and oil a 9 x 13-inch baking pan.

2. Wash the spinach, removing only the bad stems from the bunch. Drain and dry well. (If you are using frozen spinach, make sure to thaw and drain it well.)

3. Using the food processor's pulse mode, finely chop the fresh spinach and add it to a large mixing bowl. You will probably need to do this in several batches. (Add the thawed and drained frozen spinach directly to the mixing bowl.)

4. Cut the zucchini into chunks and place in the food processor. Pulse until it is well diced but not mushy. Add to the mixing bowl, and do the same with the onion.

5. Add the remaining ingredients to the mixing bowl and mix well by hand.

6. Pour the egg mixture into the prepared pan.

7. Bake the mixture for 30 to 35 minutes, or until the eggs are set and the edges begin to turn golden brown.

 Variations

⊙ Replace 1 zucchini with 1 red bell pepper (seeded and quartered), 8 ounces of asparagus or 1, 14-ounce can of artichoke hearts (drained).

⊙ Add 8 to 12 chopped sun-dried tomatoes to the mixing bowl (no need to rehydrate first) in step 5.

⊙ Substitute Swiss chard for up to half of the spinach.

Love Thy Leftovers

⊙ Prepare Spinach "Soufflé" on the weekend and eat any leftovers during the week for breakfast or lunch.

⊙ Place leftover Spinach "Soufflé" between two slices of whole grain bread or toast to make a yummy sandwich, or reheat it in a whole wheat tortilla for a breakfast burrito.

Multigrain Pancakes

Serve the pancakes with butter, *Applesauce* (page 181), *Berry Cherry Fruit Topping* (page 179), all-fruit spread or 100 percent maple syrup.

Makes about 12, 3-inch pancakes.

DRY INGREDIENTS

½ to ¾ cup pecans or walnuts

½ cup buckwheat flour

½ cup flour (whole wheat, whole spelt, oat or a combination)

⅓ cup rolled oats

2 tablespoons corn flour or cornmeal

1½ teaspoons baking powder

¼ teaspoon salt

¼ to ½ teaspoon cinnamon

WET INGREDIENTS

1¼ cups milk or rice milk

¼ cup plain yogurt or kefir

1 to 2 tablespoons extra virgin olive oil

1 tablespoon honey or maple syrup

1 egg

2 small bananas or 1 large banana, diced or sliced (optional)

1. Preheat the oven to 200 degrees.

2. Chop the nuts and combine with the remaining dry ingredients in a medium bowl.

3. In a glass measuring cup, combine the wet ingredients.

4. Pour the wet ingredients into the dry ingredients and whisk together until smooth.

5. Coat a nonstick frying pan with olive oil and heat to medium. When the pan is hot, scoop up the batter using a ¼-cup measure and pour onto the pan.

6. Cook the pancakes until tiny bubbles form on top of each, about 3 to 5 minutes. Flip the pancakes to the other side and cook until both sides are golden brown.

7. As you prepare the pancakes, put them on a cookie sheet in the oven so they stay warm.

Divine Design: Buckwheat

God created buckwheat—which is actually unrelated to wheat—to help slow the aging process, reduce blood pressure and aid in metabolism.

 Variations

⊙ Substitute 1 to 1½ cups fresh or frozen blueberries for the banana.

⊙ Add several teaspoons of flaxseed meal to the batter.

 Love Thy Leftovers

Make the pancakes on the weekend and enjoy leftovers during the week. They make a great snack: just pop them in the toaster oven, bake until warm, and spread them with butter. Or smear them with peanut butter for a quick midweek breakfast.

Peanut Butter and Banana Roll-Ups

The filling keeps well, so you can prepare it ahead of time. When you are ready to eat, just spread the filling on the tortilla and add the banana.

Makes 2 roll-ups.

Heaping ¼ cup peanut butter

¼ cup plain yogurt

2 tablespoons oat bran

2 teaspoons honey

¼ teaspoon cinnamon

Dash of salt

2 whole wheat tortillas

1 banana

1. Combine the first six ingredients (peanut butter through salt) in a small bowl. If the mixture is too dry, add a splash of juice or milk to moisten it.

2. Spread half of the peanut butter mixture over each tortilla.

3. Slice half of the banana over each tortilla.

4. Roll up the tortillas and serve with plenty of napkins.

 Divine Design: Peanuts

The closer to God's original design you can be, the better your body will feel. Take care of your body by buying natural peanut butters without added sugar, salt or fillers. The taste will please your mouth and the lack of additives will please your tummy.

Variations

⊛ Substitute flax meal for the oat bran.

⊛ Experiment with different nut butters.

⊛ Add chopped nuts or coconut to the peanut butter mixture or to the roll-ups.

⊛ Add raisins or other dried fruit to the peanut butter mixture or to the roll-ups.

⊛ Spread the peanut butter mixture (or simply peanut butter) on whole grain toast. Top with sliced banana and raisins.

⊛ Mash the banana into the peanut butter instead of slicing it.

Oat Breakfast Squares

Served hot or cold, these also make a good snack.

Makes about 9 squares.

½ cup dates or raisins (or a combination)

½ cup pecans or walnuts

1½ cups rolled oats

½ cup *Applesauce* (page 181) or store-bought applesauce

½ cup milk or rice milk

¼ cup honey or maple syrup

1 teaspoon cinnamon

Heaping ¼ teaspoon salt

1 unpeeled apple

1. Preheat the oven to 375 degrees. Oil an 8 x 8-inch baking pan or a 9-inch pie pan.

2. Chop the dates (if using) and nuts and add to a medium bowl.

3. Add the next six ingredients (oats through salt) to the bowl, mix to incorporate, and set aside.

4. Chop or shred the apple. Add to the oat mixture and mix to incorporate.

5. Press the oat mixture into the prepared pan and bake for 25 to 30 minutes. Cut into squares and serve warm or at room temperature.

 Divine Design: Oats

Eating oats—an intelligently designed low-fat grain—actually lowers cholesterol and blood pressure, and reduces your risk of heart disease.

Variations

⊚ Add ¼ to ⅓ cup dried unsweetened coconut to the dry ingredients.

⊚ Substitute plain yogurt or kefir for up to half of the applesauce.

Smoothies

Frozen fruit is the key to a good smoothie. To make sure that you have a frozen banana available, take ripe bananas that might go unused, peel them, put them in a freezer bag, and pop them into the freezer.

Makes 1 serving (about 2½ cups).

1 cup juice, milk or rice milk (or a combination)

½ cup plain yogurt

1 fresh or frozen banana

1 cup mixed, fresh or frozen fruit, such as:

- Strawberries
- Blueberries or other mixed berries
- Peach slices
- Mango slices

1. Pour the juice or milk into a blender cup. Add the yogurt.

2. Add the remaining ingredients and put the lid on the blender.

3. Turn on the blender and puree until smooth. If all the fruit is frozen, increase the blending time.

4. If your smoothie is too thick, add a little more liquid and continue blending until you reach the desired consistency. If your smoothie is too thin, add more frozen fruit (or an ice cube or two).

 Divine Design: Yogurt

Plain yogurt (a form of curds) is filled with bacteria—the good kind, called acidophilus—that keep your digestive system healthy. Yogurt's high protein content helps transform your smoothie into a complete meal, and its high calcium content protects your teeth and bones.

Variations

- Blend the milk, yogurt and frozen banana with 2 tablespoons of your favorite nut butter.
- If you do not have frozen fruit, add several ice cubes to the blender and blend until smooth.
- If you do not have a banana, use 2 cups of fresh or frozen instead of 1 cup.

Chapter 7
Desserts and Fruit

You shall have no other gods before Me." This is sobering news for those who struggle with their love for the world's most common food idol: dessert.

While both the Jewish and Christian faiths have historically turned the other cheek to food idolatry, it does not mean that God does not notice when you hold chocolate and other sweets in higher esteem than you do Him.

To be clear, God indeed created the cocoa bean, which is filled with nutrients that can boost your immune system and improve your mood. He also created honey, fruit and other natural sweeteners for us to enjoy—in moderation.

To help you appreciate the myriad of dessert foods available to you, we use chocolate sparingly in this chapter. When we do use it (as in *Chocolate Peanut Butter Balls* or *Krispy Rice Bars*), we call for semisweet chocolate chips, which contain higher amounts of God-given cocoa than milk chocolate chips do. You can also add semisweet chips to other dessert reci-

pes, such as *Almond Oat Squares* or *Carob Cake*. Speaking of carob, this naturally sweet chocolate substitute provides some folks a chocolate fix without inducing the craving that chocolate can sometimes produce.

Because of fruit's high antioxidant and fiber content (as well as its lower potential for idolatry), this chapter also emphasizes fruit-based desserts.

The sweeteners in our recipes are honey and 100 percent maple syrup, which are relatively close to God's original form and which are somewhat interchangeable. By limiting yourself to these two sweeteners, you can reduce the clutter in your pantry.

Other healthy sweeteners include brown rice syrup, agave nectar, Sucanant (cane sugar that has been dehydrated rather than boiled) and date sugar. If you experiment with these, remember that their sweetness and texture vary, so they may not be one-for-one substitutes for honey or maple syrup.

Principle 1

Hooray! God created sweet treats for you to enjoy! He gave you taste buds that enjoy sweet things, and He provided an abundance of nutrient-packed ingredients that help satisfy those cravings.

Principle 2

Moving from man-made, store-bought desserts toward Creator-based desserts is a challenging transition for some people. Your taste buds may need a little retraining before you fully enjoy these recipes, but you—and your body—will enjoy the fruits of this process.

Principle 3

When your dessert choices use God's ingredients (Principle 1), in the form He gave them to you (Principle 2), you feel more satisfied and are less prone to overindulge. Be alert for signs of "food idolatry" in your heart, mind and actions, and remember that worshipping *anything* other than God is offensive to Him.

Almond Oat Squares

This delicious dessert is a breeze to make—but it is somewhat crumbly.

Makes 9 squares.

½ cup almonds

―――――――――――

2 cups rolled oats
¼ cup oat bran
¼ cup sesame seeds
Scant ¼ teaspoon salt
½ to ⅔ cup maple syrup or honey
⅔ cup almond butter
2 tablespoons extra virgin olive oil

1. Preheat the oven to 300 degrees and oil an 8 x 8-inch baking pan.

2. Chop the almonds and combine them with the remaining ingredients in a large bowl. Mix to incorporate.

3. Transfer the oat mixture to the prepared pan and spread it evenly with a rubber spatula or a spoon. Bake for 35 minutes.

4. While the pan is still warm, cut the bars into squares.

Divine Design: Oats

God designed oats as a high-fiber grain that eases constipation and helps prevent colon cancer.

Variations

- Substitute peanuts and peanut butter, or cashews and cashew butter for the almonds and almond butter.
- Stir in ⅓ to ½ cup raisins, carob chips or semisweet chocolate chips to the batter.

Peanut Butter Fig Blondies

Makes 9 bars.

FIGS
1 cup dried figs

DRY INGREDIENTS
½ cup plus 2 tablespoons oat flour
¼ teaspoon baking powder
¼ teaspoon baking soda
Scant ¼ teaspoon salt

WET INGREDIENTS
¼ cup extra virgin olive oil
⅓ to ½ cup maple syrup or honey
½ cup peanut butter
1 egg

1. Preheat the oven to 325 degrees and oil an 8 x 8-inch baking pan.

2. Cut the stem from each fig, cut each fig into quarters, and place the cut figs into a small bowl.

3. Pour very hot tap water over the figs and allow them to sit for 10 to 15 minutes.

4. While the figs rehydrate:

   a. Combine the dry ingredients in a small bowl.

   b. Combine the wet ingredients in a medium bowl and mix well to incorporate.

5. Drain the figs, reserving 3 tablespoons of the rehydrating water. Puree the figs and reserved water in a food processor until it forms a thick paste.

6. Add the pureed figs to the wet ingredients. Mix well to incorporate.

7. Add the dry ingredients to the wet ingredients. Mix with a wooden spoon or a fork until all the ingredients are combined.

8. Evenly spread the batter into the prepared pan. Bake for 30 minutes.

9. Once the pan is cool, cut the bars into squares.

Divine Design: Figs

The Creator's design for figs includes a delectable sweetness along with a large array of health benefits. Figs can help treat various types of cancer, help prevent loss of eyesight and even help lower high blood pressure.

Variations

⊙ Substitute other dried fruit, such as raisins or apricots, for the figs.

⊙ Add ¼ cup chopped peanuts to the dry ingredients in step 4a.

Dried Cherry Nut Bars

These bars retain their shape best when kept refrigerated.

Makes 16 bars.

1½ cups whole pitted dates
1½ cups sweetened dried cherries
1 cup almonds

1. Add the dates, cherries and almonds to a food processor. Process until the mixture forms a thick paste.

2. Transfer the mixture to an 8 x 8-inch pan and spread it evenly with a rubber spatula, pressing the mixture firmly into the pan.

3. Cut the date mixture into small bars, cover the pan, and chill before serving.

Divine Design: Cherries

These fruits may take a bit of work to enjoy (removing the pits does involve some effort), but they work even harder to protect your body from disease. Cherries contain perillyl alcohol, which may help fight breast and lung cancer. So add this tiny food to your balanced diet, and make a big difference in your health.

Variations

- Substitute raisins, cranberries or other dried fruit for the cherries.
- Substitute pecans, cashews or other nuts for the almonds.
- Add several tablespoons of dried unsweetened coconut to the mixture, or press the coconut on the top.
- Add semisweet chocolate chips during step 1.

Krispy Rice Bars

Makes 9 bars.

⅓ cup sunflower seeds
⅓ cup raisins
⅓ cup dried unsweetened coconut
⅓ cup chocolate or carob chips
Scant ¼ teaspoon salt

1 cup almond butter
⅓ cup honey

3 cups crispy brown rice cereal or other
  puffed whole grain cereal

1. In a large bowl combine the first five ingredients (sunflower seeds through salt) and stir with a wooden spoon until combined.

2. In a small bowl stir together the almond butter and honey. Mix well to incorporate.

3. Pour the almond butter mixture into the large bowl with the dry ingredients and mix well to incorporate.

4. Gently fold in the rice cereal and mix well to incorporate.

5. Transfer the rice mixture to an 8 x 8-inch baking pan. Gently press the mixture into the pan and spread it evenly with a rubber spatula.

6. Cut into bars, cover the pan, and chill before serving.

 Divine Design: Sunflower Seeds

Many who struggle with depression find comfort in the Creator's natural design for sunflower seeds. These seeds contain the mood-boosting mineral selenium, which also protects you from disease.

Variation

Substitute peanut butter for the almond butter.

Oatmeal Raisin Cookies

The cookie dough will be crumbly, not doughy. But fear not: as long as the raw cookie lumps are similar in size and shape, they will bake into delicious cookies.

Makes about 30, 2-inch cookies.

DRY INGREDIENTS

½ to 1 cup walnuts or pecans

2½ cups rolled oats

1½ cups whole wheat or whole spelt flour

½ teaspoon baking soda

½ teaspoon cinnamon

¼ teaspoon salt

⅔ to 1 cup raisins

WET INGREDIENTS

¾ cup extra virgin olive oil

½ to ⅔ cup maple syrup or honey

½ teaspoon vanilla

1 egg

1. Preheat the oven to 375 degrees.

2. Chop the nuts and combine them with the other dry ingredients in a large bowl.

3. Combine the wet ingredients in a glass measuring cup.

4. Pour the wet ingredients into the dry ingredients and mix with a wooden spoon to incorporate.

5. Drop the cookie dough by teaspoonfuls onto two unoiled jelly roll pans (or cookie sheets). Slightly flatten and shape the cookies using a spoon.

6. Bake for 10 to 15 minutes. (For chewier cookies, bake for about 10 minutes. For crispier cookies, bake for about 15 minutes.)

Divine Design: Raisins

These creatively designed fruits—which are simply dried grapes—are packed with potassium. Getting a healthy dose of this mineral can help lower high blood pressure and keep your heart beating healthily.

Variations

- Substitute dried cranberries, chopped dried apricots or other dried fruit for the raisins.

- Substitute up to ½ cup oat flour for the whole wheat or whole spelt flour.

- For peanut butter oatmeal cookies, omit the cinnamon and raisins, use peanuts instead of walnuts, reduce the oil to ⅔ cup, and add ⅔ cup peanut butter to the wet ingredients.

- For oatmeal chocolate chip cookies, omit the cinnamon and substitute 1 cup semisweet chocolate chips for the raisins.

Raspberry Thumbprint Cookies

Makes about 24, 2½-inch cookies.

1 cup almonds

1 cup rolled oats

1 cup whole wheat or whole spelt flour
½ teaspoon cinnamon
Several dashes of salt
½ cup extra virgin olive oil
½ cup maple syrup

Raspberry all-fruit spread

1. Preheat the oven to 350 degrees.

2. Using a food processor, process the almonds into a crumbly flour and leave in the food processor.

3. Add the oats to the almonds and process until they become floury. Leave in the food processor.

4. Add the next five ingredients (flour through maple syrup) to the food processor and process until well incorporated.

5. Scoop the mixture by teaspoonfuls and roll into walnut-sized balls (about 1½ inches in diameter). Put each ball onto two unoiled jelly roll pans (or cookie sheets).

6. Use your thumb to make a small crater in each cookie.

7. Fill each crater with a heaping ¼ teaspoon all-fruit spread.

8. Bake the cookies for 15 to 17 minutes, or until they begin to brown slightly.

 Variations

- Use strawberry, apricot, blueberry or any other flavor of all-fruit spread.

- Substitute oat flour for some of the whole wheat flour.

Chocolate Peanut Butter Balls

These taste best when kept refrigerated.

Makes about 36, 1-inch balls.

PEANUT BUTTER BALLS

1 cup semisweet chocolate chips

½ cup flax meal

½ cup oat bran

2 tablespoons carob powder or cocoa powder

2 tablespoons dried unsweetened coconut

1 cup peanut butter

½ cup tahini

½ cup honey or maple syrup (or a combination)

¼ teaspoon salt

OPTIONAL COATINGS

- Finely chopped nuts (pecans, walnuts or peanuts)
- Dried unsweetened coconut
- Sesame seeds

1. Coarsely chop the chocolate chips and add them to a medium bowl.

2. Add the remaining peanut butter ball ingredients to the bowl and mix thoroughly until all ingredients are completely incorporated.

3. Scoop the mixture by teaspoonfuls and roll into walnut-sized balls, about 1 inch in diameter, and put on a plate or in a 9 x 13-inch baking pan.

4. If desired, roll the balls in a small dish with finely chopped nuts, coconut and/or sesame seeds.

5. Cover the plate or pan and chill before serving.

Divine Design: Chocolate

We've got good news for you! The Creator placed antioxidants called flavanols in the cocoa plant to help your body metabolize sugar and lower your blood pressure. To reap these benefits, add a bit of dark chocolate to your healthy diet. Help fix your body and your cravings.

Variations

- Press the peanut butter mixture into an 8 x 8-inch baking pan and sprinkle with the coating, rather than rolling into balls.
- Use a food processor to chop the chocolate chips. Add the remaining peanut butter ball ingredients to the food processor and process until all of the ingredients are well incorporated.
- Replace up to half of the peanut butter with almond or cashew butter.
- Substitute raisins or other dried fruit for some or all of the chocolate chips.
- Substitute carob chips for the chocolate chips.

Carob Cake

Makes 9 pieces of cake.

DRY INGREDIENTS
½ cup walnuts or pecans
1 cup oat flour
¼ cup carob powder
1 teaspoon baking powder
¼ teaspoon salt
½ cup raisins

WET INGREDIENTS
½ cup extra virgin olive oil
½ cup maple syrup or honey
¼ cup water or apple juice
2 eggs
1 teaspoon vanilla

FROSTING
3 tablespoons carob powder
3 tablespoons cashew butter
6 tablespoons maple syrup

1. Preheat the oven to 350 degrees and oil an 8 x 8-inch baking pan.

2. Chop the nuts and combine with the other dry ingredients in a medium bowl. Mix well to incorporate.

3. Combine the wet ingredients in a glass measuring cup and mix well to incorporate.

4. Add the wet ingredients to the dry ingredients. Mix with a wooden spoon or a fork until all the ingredients are well combined.

5. Pour the batter into the prepared pan. Bake for 25 to 30 minutes, or until a toothpick inserted in the middle comes out clean.

6. While the cake cools, mix together the frosting ingredients in a small bowl.

7. After the cake has cooled, spread the frosting over the cake, cut into squares, and serve.

 Divine Design: Carob

The carob is also known as "St. John's Bread," after John the Baptist, who may have been nourished by the carob—the fruit of the locust tree. The gum from its seeds is easy to digest and provides healthy fiber for your body.

Variations

◉ Use peanuts instead of walnuts or pecans, and use peanut butter instead of cashew butter for the frosting.

◉ Substitute whole wheat or whole spelt flour for the oat flour.

◉ Substitute cocoa powder for the carob powder, and substitute semisweet chocolate chips for the raisins.

◉ Stir a mashed banana into the batter before baking.

Carrot Cake

Makes about 16 servings.

DRY INGREDIENTS

4 cups whole wheat or whole spelt flour

2 tablespoons baking powder

1 teaspoon cinnamon

½ teaspoon salt

½ teaspoon ground cardamom

½ teaspoon ground nutmeg

½ cup raisins or currants

½ to ¾ cup walnuts

2 unpeeled large carrots

WET INGREDIENTS

½ cup extra virgin olive oil

1 cup maple syrup

1 cup milk or rice milk

½ cup apple juice

1 tablespoon vanilla

1. Preheat the oven to 350 degrees and oil a 9 x 13-inch baking pan.

2. Combine the first seven dry ingredients (flour through raisins) in a large bowl.

3. Chop the walnuts and shred or grate the carrots. Add to the bowl and mix to incorporate.

4. Combine the wet ingredients in a glass measuring cup.

5. Stir the liquid mixture into the dry ingredients and stir until all the ingredients are combined.

6. Pour the batter into the prepared pan. Bake for 35 to 40 minutes, or until a toothpick comes out dry and the top begins to turn light brown and crack slightly.

 Divine Design: Carrots

The intelligent design behind carrots includes not only their health benefits (they help fight emphysema, regulate blood sugar, and slow eye degeneration), but their color. Filled with beta-carotene, carrots display their bright orange hue as a signal to humans that this food is nutrient rich.

Variations

⊛ For cream cheese frosting, combine 1, 8-ounce package of cream cheese with 2 to 3 tablespoons maple syrup in a food processor and process until creamy. Frost the cake once it has cooled.

⊛ For carob frosting, combine ¼ cup carob powder, ¼ cup cashew butter and ½ cup maple syrup. Frost the cake once it has cooled.

⊛ Add ½ to 1 cup chopped pineapple to the bowl during step 5, and add up to ¼ cup chopped pineapple to the cream cheese frosting described in the first variation.

⊛ Add ¼ to ⅓ cup dried unsweetened coconut to the dry ingredients during step 2.

Pecan Pie

Makes 1, 9-inch pie (8 servings).

CRUST

½ cup almonds
½ cup rolled oats
½ cup whole wheat or whole spelt flour
¼ cup extra virgin olive oil
¼ cup maple syrup
¼ teaspoon cinnamon
Dash of salt

FILLING

2 cups pecans

4 eggs
⅔ to ¾ cup maple syrup
Juice of ½ lemon (about 2 tablespoons)
½ teaspoon cinnamon
1½ teaspoons vanilla
¼ teaspoon salt

1. Preheat the oven to 375 degrees and oil a 9-inch pie pan.

2. Prepare the pie crust:

   a. Using a food processor, process the almonds into a crumbly flour and leave in the food processor.

   b. Add the oats to the almonds in the food processor and process until the oats become floury.

   c. Add the remaining crust ingredients to the food processor and process until well incorporated.

   d. Press the pie crust into the prepared pan.

3. Chop the pecans and spread evenly over the crust.

4. Combine the remaining filling ingredients in a food processor or blender and blend until well incorporated and frothy.

5. Pour the liquid filling mixture into the pie pan and carefully put into the oven (the pan will be very full).

6. Bake for 25 to 30 minutes, or until the center of the pie is set. Let cool for about 30 minutes before serving.

Divine Design: Pecans

The next time you crave a healthy snack that won't leave you wanting more, try pecans. The Creator filled these nuts with plenty of nutrients: protein, carbohydrates, B vitamins, iron, potassium and fiber. They'll fill you up, and if you eat them unsalted and in moderate amounts, they won't fill you out.

 Love Thy Leftovers

Refrigerate any leftover pie.

Mud Pie

Make sure to soak the cashews the day before you prepare this super-easy pie.

Makes 1, 9-inch pie (8 servings).

FILLING

1 cup raw cashews

2 ripe bananas

¼ cup carob powder or unsweetened cocoa powder

½ to ⅔ cup maple syrup

Scant ¼ teaspoon salt

¾ cup peanut butter

CRUST

2½ cups pecans or walnuts (or a combination)

1½ cups whole pitted dates

TOPPING OPTIONS (CHOOSE ONE)

- 1 sliced banana
- Dried unsweetened coconut
- Chopped pecans or peanuts

1. Cover the cashews with water and soak them overnight (at least 12 hours).

2. Make the filling:

   a. Once the cashews have soaked at least 12 hours, drain them and add them to a food processor. Puree until the cashews become a crumbly flour.

   b. Add the remaining filling ingredients to the food processor and puree until creamy.

3. Make the crust:

   a. Finely chop the pecans using a food processor.

   b. Add the dates to the food processor and puree until the mixture forms a loose ball.

   c. Press the crust mixture into a 9-inch pie pan.

4. Pour the filling mixture into the pie pan and evenly spread over the crust.

5. Top the pie with a topping of your choice, cover the pan, and put in the freezer. For a softer pie, freeze for 1 to 2 hours; for a firm pie, freeze for 4 to 6 hours.

Divine Design: Cashews

Did you know God designed cashews to help prevent migraines, muscle spasms and high blood pressure? All of these benefits come with a healthy serving of magnesium. Just one-half cup of cashews provides 22 percent of the daily value of this fantastic mineral.

Easy No-Bake Cheesecake

Makes 1, 9-inch pie (8 servings).

CRUST

2½ cups walnuts or pecans (or a combination)

1½ cups whole pitted dates

FILLING

1 cup plain yogurt

1, 8-ounce package of cream cheese

¼ cup maple syrup

¼ cup all-fruit spread

1 teaspoon vanilla

Several dashes of salt

2 cups fresh fruit (such as sliced strawberries, blueberries, sliced peaches or a combination)

1. Make the crust:

   a. Combine the nuts and dates in a food processor and process until finely chopped.

   b. Evenly press the mixture into a 9-inch pie pan to form the crust.

2. Make the filling:

   a. Combine all the filling ingredients (except the fresh fruit) in a food processor and process until creamy.

   b. Stir the fruit into the yogurt mixture by hand and gently pour the mixture into the pie shell. Depending on the size of your food processor, you might need to transfer the yogurt mixture to a large mixing bowl before stirring in the fruit.

3. Cover the cheesecake and freeze for several hours before serving.

 Divine Design: Dates

The tall palm trees of the Holy Land bear heavy clusters of juicy dates. God created them to act as natural laxatives, provide your body with fiber and even fight off cancer. In both Jewish and Christian traditions, the date palm is a symbol of life. These towering plants grow near living water and are a signal to those in the dry desert that both physical and spiritual sustenance is provided by the Creator for all who seek it.

Variation

For chocolate chip cheesecake, increase the maple syrup to ½ cup, omit the all-fruit spread and the fresh fruit, and add 1 cup semisweet chocolate chips to the food processor after step 2a. Process briefly to incorporate and to chop the chips into the desired size.

Apple Pie

Makes 1, 9-inch pie (8 servings).

APPLES

5 unpeeled apples (any variety)

½ cup apple juice or water

CRUST

½ cup almonds

½ cup rolled oats

½ cup whole wheat or whole spelt flour

¼ cup extra virgin olive oil

¼ cup honey

¼ teaspoon cinnamon

Dash of salt

ADDITIONAL FILLING INGREDIENTS

2 to 4 tablespoons honey

1 to 2 teaspoons cinnamon

2 teaspoons arrowroot

¼ teaspoon ground nutmeg (optional)

1. Preheat the oven to 375 degrees and oil a 9-inch pie pan.

2. Core and thinly slice the apples.

3. In a medium or large saucepan, simmer the apples and apple juice over medium-low heat, stirring occasionally, for 20 to 30 minutes, or until they begin to soften. The cooking time will depend on how thinly you sliced the apples.

4. While the apples cook, prepare the pie crust:

   a. Using a food processor, process the almonds into a crumbly flour and leave in the food processor.

   b. Add the oats to the almonds in the food processor and process until they become floury. Leave in the food processor.

   c. Add the remaining crust ingredients to the food processor and process until well incorporated.

   d. Reserve a small handful of the crust ingredients. Set aside.

   e. Press the pie crust into the prepared pan.

5. Add the additional filling ingredients to the simmering apples. Combine well.

6. Gently pour the apples into the crust and spread evenly.

7. Crumble the reserved crust dough over the top of the apples.

8. Bake for 20 to 30 minutes, or until the apples reach the desired consistency and the crust crumbles are slightly browned.

Variations

⊚ Use sliced fresh peaches or nectarines instead of the apples. If they are very ripe, there is no need to simmer first or add any liquid; just add the additional filling ingredients.

⊚ Use 2, 16-ounce bags of frozen peaches instead of the apples.

⊚ Experiment with other fruit, such as cherries or blueberries.

Blueberry Cobbler

Makes about 8 servings.

FILLING

6 cups fresh blueberries
1 tablespoon arrowroot
Juice of ¼ lemon (about 1 tablespoon)
1½ teaspoons lemon zest

TOPPING

1 cup whole wheat or whole spelt flour
2 tablespoons cornmeal or corn flour
2 teaspoons baking powder
¼ teaspoon baking soda
¼ teaspoon salt
¼ teaspoon cinnamon

¼ cup extra virgin olive oil
¼ cup honey or maple syrup
⅓ cup kefir or plain yogurt
½ teaspoon vanilla

1. Preheat the oven to 375 degrees.

2. For the filling:

   a. Toss all of the filling ingredients together in a medium bowl until well combined.

   b. Pour the filling into an 8 x 8-inch baking pan.

   c. Bake for about 25 minutes, until the filling is hot and bubbling around the edges.

3. While the berries bake, begin to assemble the topping:

   a. In a large bowl combine the first six ingredients (flour through cinnamon). Mix to incorporate.

   b. In a separate small bowl or glass measuring cup, combine the remaining ingredients. Mix to incorporate.

4. After the berries have cooked for 25 minutes, remove them from the oven and increase the oven temperature to 425 degrees.

5. Finish assembling the topping by pouring the wet ingredients into the dry ingredients. Mix to incorporate.

6. Drop equal-sized pieces of the topping dough on top of the filling in the pan. (The dough will expand to cover much of the surface area.)

7. Bake, uncovered, for 15 to 20 minutes. The topping should be slightly browned and cooked through. Serve warm or at room temperature.

Divine Design: Blueberries

God wants you to consume blueberries because of their health benefits, so He designed them to tempt you with their beauty and sweet taste. Their colorful phytochemicals act as antioxidants—they fight cancer and heart disease, and they even help to slow aging.

 Variation

Substitute 48 ounces frozen blueberries or frozen mixed berries for the fresh blueberries.

Cherry Pear Crisp

Makes about 12 servings.

TOPPING

2 cups rolled oats

½ cup whole wheat or whole spelt flour

⅓ cup extra virgin olive oil

½ cup honey

Scant ¼ teaspoon salt

FILLING

6 unpeeled large pears (about 3 pounds)

1 bag frozen cherries (10, 12 or 16 ounces)

¼ cup honey

2 tablespoons arrowroot

2 tablespoons apple juice, lemon juice or orange juice

1 teaspoon cinnamon

¼ teaspoon ground cloves (optional)

1. Preheat the oven to 325 degrees.

2. In a medium bowl combine the topping ingredients. Mix until they begin to hold together. Set aside.

3. Core and thinly slice the pears.

4. In a large bowl combine the pears with the remaining filling ingredients. Toss well to coat the fruit.

5. Pour the filling mixture into a 9 x 13-inch baking pan and cover with the prepared topping.

6. Bake the crisp, uncovered, until the top is golden brown and the fruit is tender, about 65 to 75 minutes.

7. Serve the crisp warm or at room temperature.

Divine Design: Pears

If you worry about osteoporosis or memory loss, don't forget to eat a generous portion of pears. The mineral boron was intelligently placed into pears to prevent calcium loss in bones and to promote mental alertness and a steady memory.

Variations

⊚ Use apples instead of pears or a combination of apples and pears.

⊚ Use 7 to 9 ripe peaches (3 to 4 pounds) instead of pears and cherries. Reduce the cooking time to about 45 minutes. In this variation you can also add a few fresh strawberries or blueberries.

⊚ For strawberry rhubarb crisp, use 4 cups strawberries and 4 cups rhubarb, cut into ½-inch pieces.

⊚ For a crumblier topping, substitute granulated sugar for the honey.

⊚ Substitute cold butter for the olive oil in the topping.

Rice Pudding

Makes about 4 cups.

1 cup short-grain brown rice
3½ cups milk or rice milk
½ teaspoon salt

⅓ cup walnuts

¼ to ⅓ cup maple syrup
½ teaspoon vanilla
1 teaspoon cinnamon
⅓ cup raisins

1. Add the rice, milk and salt to a medium saucepan. Bring the mixture to a boil over medium-high heat.

2. Reduce the heat to low, cover the pan with a tightly fitting lid, and simmer for 1 hour.

3. While the rice is cooking, chop the walnuts.

4. After 1 hour, stir in the walnuts and the remaining ingredients. Simmer for an additional 10 to 15 minutes. Serve warm, cold or at room temperature.

Divine Design: Rice

The healthy fiber God put in brown rice piggybacks onto the estrogen in women's bodies. This process reduces the amount of estrogen passing through the bloodstream, which is one way God regulates hormonal imbalances that can lead to breast cancer.

 Variation

Use long-grain brown rice instead of short-grain.

 Love Thy Leftovers

Unsweetened or lightly sweetened rice pudding makes a delicious breakfast. If you think you will have leftovers, omit some or all of the maple syrup, rather than fully sweetening the whole batch. Instead, stir maple syrup into each serving, as desired.

Berry Cherry Fruit Topping

Serve this dessert topping over regular vanilla yogurt, frozen yogurt or ice cream.

Makes about 1½ cups.

1½ cups fresh or frozen mixed berries or cherries (or a combination)

½ cup red wine or grape juice

¼ cup raspberry or cherry all-fruit spread

Juice of ¼ lemon (about 1 tablespoon)

1. Combine the berries or cherries, wine and all-fruit spread in a medium saucepan over medium-high heat.

2. Bring the mixture to a boil, reduce the heat to low, and simmer for 5 to 10 minutes, stirring frequently.

3. Add the lemon juice before serving. Serve warm or at room temperature.

 Divine Design: Berries

Free radicals aren't activists from the hippie generation. These substances attack and kill invading germs. However, too much of this good thing can damage internal organs and normal cells. Although God made berries small in size, He gave them the ability to pack a big wallop to keep these free radicals under control. How? Berries' antioxidants protect you against glaucoma, vision loss, varicose veins, cancer and even high cholesterol. Now *that's* radical.

 Variations

Use apple or cranberry juice instead of wine or grape juice.

♥ Love Thy Leftovers

⊚ Serve leftover topping with *Multigrain Pancakes* (page 154).

⊚ Stir leftover topping into *Hot Oat Cereal* (page 149), *Hot Millet Cereal* (page 150) or *Creamy Brown Rice Cereal* (page 151) and heat through before serving.

Honey-Glazed Pears

Serve the pears over vanilla frozen or regular yogurt and top with chopped nuts or granola.

Makes 4 servings.

4 unpeeled pears (any variety)

¼ cup apple juice
¼ cup honey
Juice of ¼ lemon
1 teaspoon vanilla
¼ teaspoon cinnamon (optional)

1. Preheat the oven to 400 degrees.

2. Cut the pears into bite-sized chunks and place them into an 8 x 8-inch baking pan.

3. Combine the remaining ingredients in a bowl and pour over the pears.

4. Cover the pears and bake for 20 minutes.

5. Remove the cover and baste the pears with the pan juices. Bake, uncovered, for an additional 25 minutes, or until the pears are tender.

6. Serve the pears warm or at room temperature.

 Variation

Use 4 bananas instead of pears. Peel the bananas and leave whole. Bake, covered, for 20 minutes, basting once during cooking.

 Love Thy Leftovers

⊚ Top *Multigrain Pancakes* (page 154) with leftover pears.

⊚ Stir leftover pears into *Hot Oat Cereal* (page 149), *Hot Millet Cereal* (page 150) or *Creamy Brown Rice Cereal* (page 151) and heat through before serving.

Applesauce

Serve warm over frozen vanilla yogurt and top with your favorite granola. Or use it to top *Multigrain Pancakes* (page 154).

Makes about 5 cups.

8 unpeeled apples

1 cup apple juice or water

1 teaspoon cinnamon

¼ to ½ teaspoon ground cloves (optional)

¼ to ½ teaspoon ground nutmeg (optional)

¼ teaspoon ground ginger (optional)

1. Core the apples, cutting each one into eight pieces.

2. Add the apples and cooking liquid to a large pot or slow cooker.

3. Cook over low heat, covered or partially covered, until the apples fall apart, about 4 to 6 hours. Stir occasionally with a wooden spoon to break up the apples.

4. Add the remaining ingredients and serve warm.

5. This applesauce will be chunky. If you prefer a smoother applesauce, transfer it in batches to a food processor or blender and puree until it reaches the desired consistency.

 Variation

- Add up to 2 cups frozen cherries or other mixed berries during step 2.

- Substitute pears for some of the apples.

Waldorf Salad

Makes 2 to 3 cups.

2 unpeeled apples

¼ to ⅓ cup walnuts

¼ to ⅓ cup raisins
¼ cup plain yogurt
Juice of ⅛ lemon (about 1½ teaspoons)
1 to 2 teaspoons honey

1. Core the apples and cut them into bite-sized pieces.

2. Chop the walnuts.

3. Combine the apples, walnuts and remaining ingredients in a medium bowl. Mix to coat.

4. Chill before serving.

Divine Design: Apples

Don't forget the God-given peel. When a whole unpeeled apple is eaten two to three times a week, the phenols and antioxidants provide significant protection against breast cancer, cholera, heart disease and diabetes.

 Variations

- Use lemon yogurt instead of plain yogurt, lemon and honey.

- Add chopped *Basic Cooked Chicken* (page 74) and diced celery to the salad to make a tasty chicken salad.

Chapter 8
Appetizers and Snacks

DIPS AND SPREADS

Spinach and Artichoke Dip

Black Bean Dip

Roasted Vegetable Dip

White Bean Dip

Guacamole

Hummus

Roasted Garlic Spread

Olive and Sun-Dried Tomato Tapenade

BARS AND OTHER SNACKS

Cherry Almond Energy Bars

Granola Bars

Sweet and Spicy Almonds

Trail Mix

Spinach Balls

Cajun-Spiced Pumpkin Seeds

SEE ALSO . . .

In today's time-challenged society, preparing appetizers to serve to guests before a meal is a luxury few people have. While the Bible encourages you to be hospitable to others, you need not make yourself crazy with preparations. In fact, Jesus reminded Martha that her energy would be better spent focusing on God than making herself crazy in the kitchen.

Thankfully, most recipes in this chapter are simple to prepare and can also be used as meal side dishes (*Spinach Balls*), desserts (*Granola Bars* or *Cherry Almond Energy Bars*) or even part of your main course (*Hummus* or *White Bean Dip*). *Trail Mix* is a great on-the-go snack, whether you are traveling to work or around the world. Of course, if you are really in a time pinch, just spread some peanut butter on an apple or piece of celery.

How do you serve all these dips and spreads? If you crave crunchy, look for whole grain crackers or chips. You can make your own whole grain pita chips, for example, by splitting open a whole grain pita, brushing each half lightly with olive oil, cutting each half into eight wedges and baking the wedges on a cookie sheet at 375 degrees for about 10 minutes, or until crisp and slightly browned.

To increase your veggie intake, you can serve many of the dips and spreads, such as *Olive and Sun-Dried Tomato Tapenade, Hummus* or *Guacamole,* on endive leaves instead of crackers or chips, or use them as a dip for raw vegetables.

Principle 1

This chapter is called "appetizers and snacks,"
but many of the recipes can be used in your meals,
since they all include God's nutritious ingredients.

Principle 2

It is easy to fall into the store-bought trap. While it might seem like
a lot of effort to prepare what you can easily buy, hidden ingredients
in store-bought "health food" snacks might surprise you.

Principle 3

Even though homemade appetizers and snacks are
healthier than store-bought, it is not healthy to eat the whole
batch (or even fantasize about eating the whole batch).
Plan ahead and take actions that help you avoid food idolatry,
such as putting *Trail Mix* into individual serving bags or containers.

Spinach and Artichoke Dip

Makes about 2 cups.

1 garlic clove

⅓ cup mayonnaise
¼ cup Parmesan cheese
½ teaspoon salt
Several generous grindings of pepper
Dash of cayenne pepper (optional)

1, 14-ounce can of artichoke hearts packed in
  water, drained
1, 10-ounce package of frozen chopped
  spinach, thawed
3 to 4 sprigs of fresh dill

1. Finely chop the garlic in a food processor.

2. Add the mayonnaise, Parmesan cheese, salt, pepper and
   cayenne to the food processor and process until smooth.

3. Add the following to the mayonnaise mix in the food
   processor:

   a. Artichokes, drained.

   b. Spinach, thawed and thoroughly drained.

   c. Dill sprigs, coarsely chopped.

4. Pulse several times, until the artichokes are chopped but
   still slightly chunky and the spinach and dill are
   incorporated.

5. Adjust seasonings to taste and chill before serving.

 Divine Design: Artichokes

Ever eaten a thistle plant before? If you think that's impossible, just gaze at this delicious unopened flower—the artichoke.
This delectable bud comes from the plant *Cynara scolymus* and was created by God to provide vitamin C, dietary fiber and
folate for your body.

 Variation

For a hot version of this dip, add 1 cup shredded mild cheddar cheese. Bake in an 8 x 8-inch baking dish at 350 degrees for
about 30 minutes, or until the dip is bubbly. (Broil to brown slightly, if desired.)

💜 Love Thy Leftovers

Use leftover dip as a sandwich spread.

Black Bean Dip

Black bean dip can be used as an appetizer (with veggies or corn tortilla chips) or as part of a meatless main: add it to a whole wheat tortilla and top with salsa, black olives and chopped green onions.

Makes about 2 cups.

1 red bell pepper
Extra virgin olive oil

1, 15-ounce can of black beans, rinsed and drained

1 garlic clove
1 tablespoon extra virgin olive oil
1½ teaspoons ground cumin
Juice of 1 lime (about 2 tablespoons)
¼ bunch cilantro (mostly leaves)
Heaping ¼ teaspoon salt
Several generous grindings of pepper
Dash of cayenne pepper

1. Preheat the oven to 400 degrees.

2. Seed the pepper and cut it into 3 or 4 large pieces.

3. Lightly coat the pepper with olive oil, place it in an 8 x 8-inch baking pan, and bake for 30 to 40 minutes, until the pepper is very soft and slightly browned.

4. Remove the pepper from the oven and cool slightly.

5. Rinse and drain the beans.

6. Add the pepper, beans and remaining ingredients to a food processor and puree until smooth. (The dip will be very thick and full of different-colored speckles.)

7. Add additional seasonings to taste.

 Divine Design: Black Beans

Even diabetes and hypoglycemia can't escape from the ingredients in God's natural medicine cabinet. The black bean's soluble fiber helps your body slowly process the bean's own carbohydrates. This provides a steady energy supply, while helping to stabilize your body's blood sugar levels.

Variations

⊛ Stir in a chopped small tomato after pureeing.

☺ Add ¼ seeded jalapeño to the food processor in step 6.

Roasted Vegetable Dip

This mixture can be used as a dip for vegetables, a sandwich spread or a brown rice topper.

Makes about 2½ cups.

1 red onion
2 small zucchini
1 yellow or red bell pepper
1 cup grape or cherry tomatoes
3 garlic cloves
2 tablespoons extra virgin olive oil

Juice of ¼ lemon (about 1 tablespoon)
⅓ cup firmly packed fresh basil leaves
½ teaspoon salt
Several generous grindings of pepper
Dash of cayenne pepper

1. Preheat the oven to 400 degrees.

2. Thickly slice the onion, cut the zucchini into ½-inch pieces, coarsely chop the pepper, quarter the tomatoes, and cut the garlic cloves in half. Add the vegetables to a 9 x 13-inch baking pan.

3. Add the olive oil to the baking pan and toss well to coat the vegetables.

4. Bake for 30 to 40 minutes, stirring once after 20 minutes. The vegetables should be very soft and slightly browned.

5. Remove the vegetables from the oven and cool slightly. Puree in a blender or food processor with the remaining ingredients, adjusting salt and lemon juice to taste. The dip will be very thick and full of different-colored speckles. Serve warm or at room temperature.

 Variations

- Substitute balsamic vinegar for the lemon juice.
- Substitute 1 large garlic clove (raw) for the 3 roasted ones.

 Love Thy Leftovers

- Use as a salsa substitute with chips and veggies, or in place of salsa in *Basic Scrambled Eggs* (page 152) or *Quesadillas* (page 111).
- Experiment with adding olive oil and balsamic vinegar to leftover dip to make a roasted vegetable salad dressing.

White Bean Dip

Makes about 2 cups.

1 garlic clove

1, 15-ounce can of white beans, rinsed and drained

2 tablespoons extra virgin olive oil

Juice of ¼ lemon (about 1 tablespoon)

1 tablespoon red wine vinegar

1 teaspoon dried dill

1 teaspoon dried oregano

1 teaspoon Dijon mustard

¼ teaspoon salt

Several generous grindings of pepper

1. Finely chop the garlic in a food processor.

2. Rinse and drain the beans and add them to the food processor, along with the remaining ingredients. Process until smooth.

3. Add additional seasonings to taste.

 Variations

Experiment by adding one or more of the following ingredients to the food processor in step 2: kalamata olives, roasted red peppers, fresh basil, pine nuts, feta cheese, *Pesto* page (33) or capers.

Guacamole

Makes about 2 cups.

2 ripe avocados

½ medium onion or 3 green onions (white and some green)

½ cup grape or cherry tomatoes (or ½ medium tomato)

Up to ⅓ bunch cilantro (mostly leaves)

Juice of ½ lemon or 1 lime (or a combination; about 2 tablespoons)

¼ teaspoon salt

Several generous grindings of pepper

OPTIONAL INGREDIENTS
- Dash of cayenne pepper
- Dash of ground cumin
- 1 finely minced garlic clove

1. Cut the avocados in half, remove the pits, and scoop the flesh into a medium bowl. (Reserve the pits—see Love Thy Leftovers.)

2. With a fork or potato masher, mash the avocados.

3. Finely dice the onion and add it to the bowl.

4. Quarter the grape tomatoes (or finely dice the tomato) and add them to the bowl.

5. Finely chop the cilantro and add the desired amount to the bowl.

6. Add the lemon juice, salt, pepper and any optional ingredients to the bowl and mix to combine.

7. Continue mixing and mashing until you reach the desired consistency. Add additional seasonings to taste.

Divine Design: Avocados

This green fruit is a team player. When eaten with vegetables, avocados not only add taste and texture, but they also increase your body's ability to absorb important carotenoids from the vegetables. These carotenoids protect you from sickness by strengthening your immune system.

Variations

- Super-simple variation: Just add 2 to 4 tablespoons of your favorite salsa to the 2 mashed avocados.

- Add a finely diced jalapeño or other hot pepper.

- Experiment by adding corn kernels or ½ green bell pepper, finely diced.

- To extend the guacamole's life and for a creamier texture, add a dollop of plain yogurt during step 7.

Love Thy Leftovers

To prevent guacamole from turning brown, save the avocado pits and add them to the leftover guacamole. God miraculously designed the pits in such a way that they help prevent the avocado flesh from going bad too quickly.

Hummus

Hummus makes a great appetizer and snack, but it can also make a great meal: serve it with cut vegetables and whole grain crackers, or spread it on a whole wheat tortilla and top it with chopped vegetables or *Basic Roasted Vegetables* (page 15).

Makes about 2 cups.

1 to 2 garlic cloves

1, 15-ounce can of garbanzo beans, rinsed and drained

Juice of ½ lemon (about 2 tablespoons)

¼ cup tahini

1 tablespoon extra virgin olive oil

¼ to ½ teaspoon ground cumin

¼ to ½ teaspoon salt

Dash of cayenne pepper (optional)

Several generous grindings of pepper (optional)

1. Finely chop the garlic using a food processor.

2. Rinse and drain the beans. Add the beans to the food processor, along with the remaining ingredients. Process until the mixture forms a thick paste.

3. With the blade running, drizzle water into the food processor, 1 tablespoon at a time, until the mixture reaches the desired consistency.

Divine Design: Garbanzo Beans

Go straight to God's ingredients for your daily energy. Garbanzo beans are filled with fiber to help stabilize blood sugar levels, iron to keep you energized and manganese to help produce energy efficiently.

Variations

- Experiment with other ingredients, such as ground coriander, pine nuts, fresh herbs, paprika, green onions or roasted red peppers.

- Use black beans instead of garbanzo beans.

- Add a cooked, peeled eggplant during step 2 and double the other ingredients (except the beans—just use 1 can).

Roasted Garlic Spread

Use roasted garlic as a dip for vegetables or crackers, spread it on a roasted vegetable sandwich, or use it as a base layer for *Polenta Pizza* (page 52).

Makes 1 head of roasted garlic.

1 head of garlic

Extra virgin olive oil

Several dashes of salt

Parmesan cheese (optional)

1. Preheat the oven to 350 degrees.

2. Brush off the head of garlic and remove any loose outer layers (but do not peel). Cut off the end opposite the root end.

3. Place the garlic on a piece of foil, cut side up. Drizzle with olive oil (about 2 teaspoons) and salt.

4. Wrap the garlic in the foil and bake for 1 hour. The garlic is done when you can easily squeeze it out of its shell.

5. Mix the garlic pulp with additional olive oil, salt and Parmesan cheese (if using) to taste.

Divine Design: Garlic

One of God's best medicines is garlic. Adding this intelligent ingredient to your recipes can help your body fight off ear infections, lower your cholesterol and even prevent heart disease and strokes.

 Love Thy Leftovers

⊛ Add leftover cloves of roasted garlic to *Guacamole* (page 191) or *Mix and Match Salad* (page 10).

⊛ Roast 2 heads of garlic and use the leftover one to make a chunky roasted garlic vinaigrette. After squeezing out the garlic, combine it in a food processor or blender with 2 tablespoons white wine vinegar, juice of ¼ lemon (about 1 tablespoon), 1 teaspoon Dijon mustard, ¼ teaspoon salt and several generous grindings of pepper until smooth. Then, while the food processor is running, slowly pour in ⅓ cup olive oil and blend until fully incorporated.

Olive and Sun-Dried Tomato Tapenade

Use tapenade as a dip for fresh vegetables or crackers, or spread it on a roasted vegetable or other sandwich.

Makes about 1 cup.

12 sun-dried tomatoes

1 to 2 garlic cloves
1 sprig of fresh rosemary (optional)

1 cup kalamata olives
3 tablespoons capers
Zest of 1 lemon
4 teaspoons extra virgin olive oil
4 teaspoons pine nuts
2 teaspoons water

1. Add the sun-dried tomatoes to a small bowl and cover them with very hot tap water. Let stand 10 to 15 minutes, or until soft. (If you are using oil-packed sun-dried tomatoes, there is no need to soak them; just shake off the excess oil before using.)

2. When the tomatoes are soft, drain them and chop into small pieces.

3. Finely chop the garlic and rosemary (if using) in a food processor.

4. Add the remaining ingredients and process until the tapenade reaches the desired consistency.

 Divine Design: Olives

Did you know that black olives are actually very ripe green ones? Both colors reap the same great benefits: God packed olives with vitamin E, which helps stop damage to cells—preventing cancer.

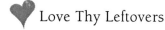 Variation

Substitute roasted red peppers for the sun-dried tomatoes.

Love Thy Leftovers

⊛ Spread over uncooked chicken or fish and cook according to the directions for *Basic Cooked Chicken* (page 74) or *Basic Cooked Fish* (page 63), or use as a topping for either one after cooking.

⊛ Toss leftover tapenade with some steamed cauliflower from *Cauliflower Salad with Sun-Dried Tomatoes and Olives* (page 13).

⊛ Use as a sauce in *Mix and Match Whole Grain Pasta* (page 46).

Cherry Almond Energy Bars

You can also prepare this recipe in the food processor. Follow the steps indicated without transferring the ingredients to another bowl.

Makes 16 bars.

½ cup almonds
½ cup pumpkin seeds
½ cup dried unsweetened coconut
½ cup carob powder
6 tablespoons sesame seeds

½ cup almond butter
¼ cup honey
¼ cup cherry all-fruit spread

1. Finely grind the almonds in a food processor and add to a medium mixing bowl.

2. Grind the pumpkin seeds in a food processor and add to the bowl. They do not need to be as finely ground as the almonds.

3. Grind the coconut in a food processor until it's the consistency of the sesame seeds and add to the bowl.

4. Add the carob powder and sesame seeds to the bowl and mix to incorporate.

5. Add the remaining ingredients to the mixing bowl. Mix well to incorporate.

6. Press the mixture into an 8 x 8-inch baking pan. (The mixture may seem dry and crumbly at first, but it will become a firm paste once you press it into the pan.) Cut into 16, 2x2-inch bars. Cover with foil and freeze before serving. The bars taste best when served frozen.

Divine Design: Carob

Could the carob be the forbidden fruit in the Garden of Eden? Its name comes from a Hebrew root meaning "destruction." Even if it was once forbidden, God does not now forbid you to eat this wild fruit, whose nectar yields delicious honey to tantalize your taste buds.

Variations

⊚ Substitute cashews and cashew butter, or peanuts and peanut butter for the almonds and almond butter.

⊚ Experiment with different all-fruit spreads, such as raspberry or apricot, instead of cherry.

⊚ Experiment with using unsweetened cocoa powder instead of the carob powder.

Granola Bars

Makes 9 bars.

DRY INGREDIENTS

⅓ cup walnuts

1½ cups granola (homemade or store-bought)

1 cup rolled oats

¾ cup dried fruit, such as raisins, cranberries or cherries

½ cup oat flour

½ teaspoon cinnamon

WET INGREDIENTS

2 eggs

⅓ cup honey or maple syrup

2 tablespoons extra virgin olive oil

1. Preheat the oven to 350 degrees and generously oil an 8 x 8-inch baking pan.

2. Chop the walnuts and add to a large bowl.

3. Add the remaining dry ingredients to the bowl and mix to incorporate.

4. In a separate bowl combine the wet ingredients and mix to incorporate.

5. Pour the egg mixture into the granola mixture and stir until all the ingredients are coated. Press the mixture evenly into the prepared pan.

6. Bake for 20 to 25 minutes, or until light brown.

7. While the pan is still warm, cut into 9 squares.

 Variations

⊙ For a dessert, increase the honey to ½ to ⅔ cup.

⊙ Experiment with other dried fruit, such as chopped apricots, dates or plums (prunes).

⊙ Experiment with different nuts, such as pecans, almonds or peanuts.

 Love Thy Leftovers

⊙ Crumble granola bars on top of *Honey-Glazed Pears* (page 180).

⊙ Eat leftover granola bars for breakfast.

Sweet and Spicy Almonds

Makes about 4 cups.

4 tablespoons butter

6 tablespoons maple syrup

2 teaspoons salt (1½ teaspoons if you are using salted butter)

1 teaspoon ground cumin

1 teaspoon cinnamon

¼ teaspoon cayenne pepper

3 cups almonds

1 cup dried cranberries or cherries

1. Preheat the oven to 325 degrees and line a jelly roll pan with foil or parchment paper.

2. Melt the butter in a medium saucepan over medium heat.

3. Reduce the heat to low and add the next five ingredients (maple syrup through cayenne). Mix to incorporate.

4. Add the almonds to the saucepan and mix until the almonds are evenly coated in the butter mixture.

5. Evenly spread the almonds onto the jelly roll pan.

6. Bake the almonds for 10 minutes and stir. Then bake the almonds for an additional 10 minutes.

7. Stir the cranberries into the almonds and bake for an additional 2 minutes.

8. Remove the almonds from the oven and transfer them to a clean foil-lined or paper-lined jelly roll pan or 9 x 13-inch baking pan. Make sure to break apart any clumps as they cool.

 Divine Design: Almonds

God told the prophet Jeremiah, as he saw a vision of an almond tree branch, that He watched over His Word to accomplish it. He also watches over how you nourish your body. He created the almond, which is high in healthy (monounsaturated) fats. When eaten in a balanced diet, the almond promotes weight loss and low cholesterol. His watchful care is everywhere.

Variation

Substitute raisins for the cranberries.

Trail Mix

Put whatever you want in your trail mix—just use equal parts of each. Your ingredients can be simple; for example, you can use only almonds, pumpkin seeds and dried cranberries. But we think this recipe tastes the best when we use a wide variety of ingredients.

Makes about 1½ cups.

½ cup mixed nuts, such as:
- Walnuts
- Almonds
- Pecans

½ cup mixed, large seeds, such as:
- Pumpkin
- Sunflower

½ to 1 cup mixed, dried fruit, such as:
- Raisins
- Apricots
- Cranberries

Several dashes of salt (if none of the nuts or seeds have salt)

1. Mix the ingredients together in a plastic container or a plastic zipper bag.

 Variations

- Experiment with other nuts, such as cashews, peanuts, pistachios, Brazil nuts or hazelnuts.
- Experiment with other dried fruit, such as banana chips, blueberries, cherries or chopped dates.
- Add a scoop of granola to the trail mix.
- Add semisweet chocolate chips or carob chips to the trail mix.

 Love Thy Leftovers

Use extra trail mix as a topping for yogurt, or eat it for breakfast.

Spinach Balls

Using a food processor helps simplify this recipe's preparation. Serve with *Marinara Sauce* (page 32) or other pasta sauce.

Makes about 30, 1-inch balls.

1 medium onion

2 garlic cloves

Extra virgin olive oil

2, 10-ounce packages of frozen chopped spinach, thawed

1 slice of whole grain bread (or ¼ cup bread crumbs)

⅓ cup Parmesan cheese

1 egg

½ teaspoon salt

Several generous grindings of pepper

1. Finely chop the onion and garlic.

2. Coat the bottom of a large frying pan with olive oil (about 2 tablespoons) and sauté the onions and garlic over medium-high heat. While the onions and garlic cook:

   a. Thoroughly drain the liquid from the spinach and add it to a large bowl.

   b. Add the bread to a food processor and process to make bread crumbs. Add to the bowl.

3. When the onions and garlic are soft (5 to 10 minutes), add them to the bowl along with the remaining ingredients. Mix well to incorporate.

4. Preheat the oven to 350 degrees and oil a jelly roll pan (or cookie sheet).

5. Form the spinach mixture into walnut-sized balls (about 1 inch in diameter) and arrange them on the prepared pan.

6. Bake for 30 minutes. Serve hot, warm or at room temperature.

 Divine Design: Spinach

Perhaps the healthiest ingredients in God's creation, leafy green vegetables such as spinach are bursting with nutrients. For instance: one cup of cooked spinach contains over 1,000 percent of the recommended daily amount of vitamin K, a key nutrient for promoting bone health and stability.

♥ Love Thy Leftovers

Gently add leftover spinach balls to *Mix and Match Whole Grain Pasta* (page 46).

Cajun-Spiced Pumpkin Seeds

Makes 1½ cups.

CAJUN SPICE MIX

2½ tablespoons paprika

1 tablespoon dried thyme

1 tablespoon dried oregano

½ tablespoon ground cumin

½ tablespoon onion powder

1 tablespoon garlic powder

1 tablespoon dried basil

½ teaspoon cayenne pepper

1 tablespoon salt

Lots of fresh ground pepper
 (½ to 1 tablespoon)

PUMPKIN SEEDS

1½ cups pumpkin seeds

2 teaspoons olive oil

1. Preheat the oven to 300 degrees.

2. Combine the Cajun Spice Mix ingredients in a small jar and mix well to combine.

3. In a medium bowl toss the pumpkin seeds with the olive oil and 2 tablespoons Cajun Spice Mix to evenly coat.

4. Place the seeds on a jelly roll pan, making sure they are in a single layer.

5. Bake for 15 to 20 minutes. The seeds will begin to turn slightly golden and "pop" when they are done.

 Variations

- Sprinkle Cajun Spice Mix on popcorn.

- Instead of store-bought pumpkin seeds, use the seeds that you would otherwise discard when making *Spaghetti Squash* (page 20), *Maple Walnut Acorn Squash* (page 16) or *"Cream" of Squash Soup* (page 129). To prepare the seeds, simply separate the seeds from the stringy stuff, wash the seeds, pat the seeds dry with a paper towel, and use the seeds in step 3. Increase the cooking time to 20 to 30 minutes.

 Love Thy Leftovers

- Use leftover Cajun-Spiced Pumpkin Seeds as a salad topper in a *Mix and Match Salad* (page 10).

- Sprinkle the seeds on chili or baked potatoes.

- Use the remaining spice mix to blacken fish or chicken, to mix into the marinade for *Basic Cooked Chicken* (page 74), or to season *Basic Roasted Potatoes* (page 53) or *Sweet Potato Fries* (page 21) before baking.

Appendix A
Leviticus Chapter 11 (NASB)

Lev. 11:1

The LORD spoke again to Moses and to Aaron, saying to them, 2 "Speak to the sons of Israel, saying, 'These are the creatures which you may eat from all the animals that are on the earth. 3 'Whatever divides a hoof, thus making split hoofs, and chews the cud, among the animals, that you may eat. 4 'Nevertheless, you are not to eat of these, among those which chew the cud, or among those which divide the hoof: the camel, for though it chews cud, it does not divide the hoof, it is unclean to you. 5 'Likewise, the rock badger, for though it chews cud, it does not divide the hoof, it is unclean to you; 6 the rabbit also, for though it chews cud, it does not divide the hoof, it is unclean to you; 7 and the pig, for though it divides the hoof, thus making a split hoof, it does not chew cud, it is unclean to you. 8 'You shall not eat of their flesh nor touch their carcasses; they are unclean to you.

Lev. 11:9

'These you may eat, whatever is in the water: all that have fins and scales, those in the water, in the seas or in the rivers, you may eat. 10 'But whatever is in the seas and in the rivers, that do not have fins and scales among all the teeming life of the water, and among all the living creatures that are in the water, they are detestable things to you, 11 and they shall be abhorrent to you; you may not eat of their flesh, and their carcasses you shall detest. 12 'Whatever in the water does not have fins and scales is abhorrent to you.

Lev. 11:13

'These, moreover, you shall detest among the birds; they are abhorrent, not to be eaten: the eagle and the vulture and the buzzard, 14 and the kite and the falcon in its kind, 15 every raven in its kind, 16 and the ostrich and the owl and the sea gull and the hawk in its kind, 17 and the little owl and the cormorant and the great owl, 18 and the white owl and the pelican and the carrion vulture, 19 and the stork, the heron in its kinds, and the hoopoe, and the bat.

Lev. 11:20

'All the winged insects that walk on all fours are detestable to you. 21 'Yet these you may eat among all the winged insects which walk on all fours: those which have above their feet jointed legs with which to jump on the earth. 22 'These of them you may eat: the locust in its kinds, and the devastating locust in its kinds, and the cricket in its kinds, and the grasshopper in its kinds. 23 'But all other winged insects which are four-footed are detestable to you.

Lev. 11:24

'By these, moreover, you will be made unclean: whoever touches their carcasses becomes unclean until evening, 25 and whoever picks up any of their carcasses shall wash his clothes and be unclean until evening. 26 'Concerning all the animals which divide the hoof, but do not make a split hoof, or which do not chew cud, they are unclean to you: whoever touches them becomes unclean. 27 'Also whatever walks on its paws, among all the creatures that walk on all fours, are unclean to you; whoever touches their carcasses becomes unclean until evening, 28 and the one who picks up their carcasses shall wash his clothes and be unclean until evening; they are unclean to you.

Lev. 11:29

'Now these are to you the unclean among the swarming things which swarm on the earth: the mole, and the mouse, and the great lizard in its kinds, 30 and the gecko, and the crocodile, and the lizard, and the sand reptile, and the chameleon. 31 'These are to you the unclean among all the swarming things; whoever touches them when they are dead becomes unclean until evening. 32 'Also anything on which one of them may fall when they are dead, becomes unclean, including any wooden article, or clothing,

or a skin, or a sack—any article of which use is made—it shall be put in the water and be unclean until evening, then it becomes clean. 33 'As for any earthenware vessel into which one of them may fall, whatever is in it becomes unclean and you shall break the vessel. 34 'Any of the food which may be eaten, on which water comes, shall become unclean; and any liquid which may be drunk in every vessel shall become unclean. 35 'Everything, moreover, on which part of their carcass may fall becomes unclean; an oven or a stove shall be smashed; they are unclean and shall continue as unclean to you. 36 'Nevertheless a spring or a cistern collecting water shall be clean, though the one who touches their carcass shall be unclean. 37 'And if a part of their carcass falls on any seed for sowing which is to be sown, it is clean. 38 'Though if water is put on the seed, and a part of their carcass falls on it, it is unclean to you.

Lev. 11:39

'Also if one of the animals dies which you have for food, the one who touches its carcass becomes unclean until evening. 40 'He too, who eats some of its carcass shall wash his clothes and be unclean until evening; and the one who picks up its carcass shall wash his clothes and be unclean until evening.

Lev. 11:41

'Now every swarming thing that swarms on the earth is detestable, not to be eaten. 42 'Whatever crawls on its belly, and whatever walks on all fours, whatever has many feet, in respect to every swarming thing that swarms on the earth, you shall not eat them, for they are detestable. 43 'Do not render yourselves detestable through any of the swarming things that swarm; and you shall not make yourselves unclean with them so that you become unclean. 44 'For I am the LORD your God. Consecrate yourselves therefore, and be holy; for I am holy. And you shall not make yourselves unclean with any of the swarming things that swarm on the earth. 45 'For I am the LORD, who brought you up from the land of Egypt, to be your God; thus you shall be holy for I am holy.'"

Lev. 11:46

This is the law regarding the animal, and the bird, and every living thing that moves in the waters, and everything that swarms on the earth, 47 to make a distinction between the unclean and the clean, and between the edible creature and the creature which is not to be eaten.

Appendix B
Lists of Clean and Unclean Meats

CLEAN ANIMALS

Animals That Chew the Cud and Part the Hoof

Antelope
Bison (buffalo)
Caribou
Cattle (beef, veal)
Deer (venison)
Elk
Gazelle
Giraffe
Goat
Hart
Ibex
Moose
Ox
Reindeer
Sheep (lamb, mutton)

Fish with Fins and Scales

Anchovy
Barracuda
Bass
Black pomfret (monchong)
Bluefish
Bluegill

Carp
Cod
Crappie
Drum
Flounder
Grouper
Grunt
Haddock
Hake
Halibut
Hardhead
Herring (alewife)
Kingfish
Mackerel (cobia)
Mahi-mahi (dorado, dolphin-fish; not to be confused with the mammal dolphin)
Minnow
Mullet
Perch (bream)
Pike (pickerel, jack)
Pollock (Boston bluefish)
Rockfish
Salmon
Sardine (pilchard)
Shad
Silver hake (whiting)

Smelt (frost fish, ice fish)
Snapper (ebu, jobfish, lehi, onaga, opakapaka, uku)
Sole
Steelhead
Sucker
Sunfish
Tarpon
Trout (weakfish)
Tuna (ahi, aku, albacore, bonito, tombo)
Turbot (except European turbot)
Whitefish

Birds with Clean Characteristics

Chicken
Dove
Duck
Goose
Grouse
Guinea fowl
Partridge
Peafowl
Pheasant
Pigeon

Prairie chicken

Ptarmigan

Quail

Sage hen

Sparrow (and other song-
 birds)

Swan*

Teal

Turkey

Insects

Types of locusts that may
 include crickets and
 grasshoppers

* In the King James Version,
 Leviticus 11:18 and
 Deuteronomy 14:16 list "swan"
 among unclean birds. However,
 this seems to be a mistranslation.
 The original word apparently
 refers to a kind of owl and is so
 translated in most modern Bible
 versions.

UNCLEAN ANIMALS

Animals with Unclean Characteristics

Swine

Boar

Peccary

Pig (hog, bacon, ham, lard,
 pork, most sausage and
 pepperoni)

Canines

Coyote

Dog

Fox

Hyena

Jackal

Wolf

Felines

Cat

Cheetah

Leopard

Lion

Panther

Tiger

Equines

Ass

Donkey

Horse

Mule

Onager

Zebra (quagga)

Other

Armadillo

Badger

Bear

Beaver

Camel

Elephant

Gorilla

Groundhog

Hare

Hippopotamus

Kangaroo

Llama (alpaca, vicuña)

Mole

Monkey

Mouse

Muskrat

Opossum

Porcupine

Rabbit

Raccoon

Rat

Rhinoceros

Skunk

Slug

Snail (escargot)

Squirrel

Wallaby

Weasel

Wolverine

Worm

All insects except some in the
 locust family

Marine Animals Without Scales and Fins

Fish

Bullhead
Catfish
Eel
European turbot
Marlin
Paddlefish
Shark
Stickleback
Squid
Sturgeon (includes most caviar)
Swordfish

Shellfish

Abalone
Clam
Crab
Crayfish
Lobster
Mussel
Prawn
Oyster
Scallop
Shrimp

Soft Body

Cuttlefish
Jellyfish
Limpet
Octopus
Squid (calamari)

Sea Mammals

Dolphin
Otter
Porpoise
Seal
Walrus
Whale

Birds of Prey, Scavengers and Others

Albatross
Bat
Bittern
Buzzard
Condor
Coot
Cormorant
Crane
Crow
Cuckoo
Eagle
Flamingo
Grebe
Grosbeak
Gull
Hawk
Heron
Kite
Lapwing
Loon
Magpie
Osprey
Ostrich
Owl
Parrot
Pelican
Penguin
Plover
Rail
Raven
Roadrunner
Sandpiper
Seagull
Stork
Swallow
Swift
Vulture
Water hen
Woodpecker

Reptiles

Alligator
Caiman
Crocodile
Lizard
Snake
Turtle

Amphibians

Blindworm
Frog
Newt
Salamander
Toad

Reprinted by permission of United Church of God, *an International Association,* "What Does the Bible Teach about Clean and Unclean Meats?" www.ucg.org/booklets/CU.

Index

Our Stories:
Hope Egan

Most of my childhood memories revolve around food: Chasing after the ice cream truck's bells like Pavlov's dog. Snooping for Pop-Tarts after Mom bought groceries. Eating pizza topped with crushed potato chips in the grade school cafeteria.

I didn't think too much about it, though, until 1990 when I visited my mom in a thirty-day, twelve-step-based inpatient treatment center for food addiction. There I learned about compulsive eating—the kind that cripples the heart, the mind and the soul, as well as the body. I immediately understood that this wasn't just Mom's problem—it was mine too.

For several years I avoided twelve-step groups to address my compulsive eating. Why? Because God was their solution.

God? Didn't He have anything better to do than keep me from eating another Matt's Chocolate Chip Cookie? I had always thought that He disappeared after freeing the slaves from Egypt and parting the Red Sea. (*The Ten Commandments* movie was an integral part of my childhood faith formation.) Turning to God for help was not an option I seriously considered.

My preoccupation with food continued and I eventually hit bottom. In 1992 a car accident on Thanksgiving meant that I couldn't exercise. In danger of packing on the pounds, I confessed my fear to my therapist. She affirmed that three trips a day to the candy machine for Reese's Peanut Butter Cups was not normal, and she urged me to go to Overeaters Anonymous (OA).

Where did I get my goofy eating habits?

Raised by a health food nut mom and a junk-food junkie dad, I naturally developed confused eating patterns. My taste buds craved Dad's chocolate cake, but when I'd unpack my sack lunch, I was always disappointed to find Mom's carrot sticks and tuna sandwiches on whole wheat bread.

In college and beyond, the floodgates opened to years of pent-up sugar demand: I rejoiced in Gummi Bears and cookies galore. I cycled between healthy and crazy eating, always using rigorous exercise to support my sugar habit.

Back to my therapist. Still skeptical (but desperate), I listened to her and attended my first OA meeting in January 1993, where I learned more about food addiction. How, for example, could someone like my mom eat so much "healthy" food but still have an unhealthy relationship with it? I learned that food idolatry is an internal issue—both emotional and spiritual—that affects many people, regardless of what they look like and regardless of how "healthy" they are eating.

What really struck me at these OA meetings, though, was the emphasis on God. I was surprised by how "normal" the God-focused OA people seemed. In spite of their stories about how God had changed their lives, I decided to be my own "higher power." Not surprisingly, my life got worse.

One evening, after a particularly gut-wrenching phone conversation with my mom, I broke down and sobbed. Why was I always so mean to her? I realized that I needed serious help, so I begged God to restore my life to sanity. (Besides my crazy eating, I had virtually no success with family or romantic relationships, and I was a borderline compulsive shopper.)

After taking that leap of faith, my food obsession surprisingly began to ease and I abstained from eating sugar for longer than I ever had. But while my food choices improved, my relationships with God and with other people were still inadequate.

Having been raised in a secular Jewish home, I just assumed that it was the God of Abraham, Isaac and Jacob who I sought. But I eventually wondered about Jesus. After all, in spite of living in a predominantly Christian culture, I didn't really know anything about this supposed messiah. I was curious to learn about Him, so I did some reading. My research made me think that Jesus might not be such a bad guy after all.

After trying to "turn my life over to God" for three years—but still not really knowing Him—I went to Safe Place, a small Christian faith community that was an offshoot of Park Community Church in Chicago.

I was fascinated to learn about the God of Abraham from the Bible's perspective. Familiar stories like Adam and Eve, Noah's Ark, and Joseph (of Technicolor Dreamcoat fame) were actually woven together as part of God's bigger story. I even learned the answer to The Question that had nagged me since childhood: "And then what happened? Where did He go?" I was relieved to learn that His story continued to unfold and that He was alive and well and still working in people's lives, thousands of years later.

I loved being part of this faith community that took God so seriously; my perspective on this topic had, obviously, radically changed. And the Christian teachings about relationships and living life were so compelling that I began to think maybe Jesus was The One. Who else could have inspired such wisdom about marriage, dating and sex? I eventually couldn't help myself: I became a committed follower of Jesus.

Oy! What was a nice Jewish girl like me doing following Jesus? It seemed odd, but the more I committed myself, the more my food compulsions eased and the better my relationships became. My lifelong bumpy ride was finally starting to smooth out.

Then I found out I had candida, a systemic yeast infection that infiltrates the entire bloodstream and whose treatment is a strict diet. How strict? Let's just say that it's easier to list what I could eat than what I couldn't: fruits, vegetables, nuts, seeds, beans, certain whole grains, fish and chicken. How would I survive without sugar, dairy, wheat, yeast or processed foods?

I cried for days when I learned that I'd have to fix three meals a day—from scratch—for at least three months! The thought of cooking for real, for every meal, sounded tedious and tasteless, and I didn't know where to start, especially since my cooking repertoire was limited to eggs, pancakes, cookies and macaroni and cheese.

How did I survive this long without knowing how to cook? Salad bars and frozen dinners. Simple cheese sandwiches. Dinners out with friends. An occasional pizza delivery. My diet was certainly not as bad as in my pre-OA days (grazing all day on a box of chocolate crumb donuts) and possibly healthier than the average American's. But my diet was far from ideal.

Several books on eliminating yeast from my diet motivated me to prepare three wholesome meals a day, even though I could barely boil water when I began. In spite of the cooking trauma, candida turned out to be a huge gift. Not only did I learn how to cook, but I looked better and felt healthier than ever. By the time I was healed, I enjoyed my home cooking more than eating out!

Even with the blessings, I wasn't sure what to do next. Did I have to eat healthy forever? It obviously couldn't hurt, but the "candida diet" did get tiresome. And more importantly, what did God think about all this?

By this point I had fully committed my life to the God of the Bible, which meant seeking His guidance in all areas of my life. But what, exactly, did He think about my food? From my experiences in the Christian church, it seemed like celebrating with rich desserts and avoiding fruits and vegetables was the norm. And pork—something the Bible frowns on—was usually served on religious holidays like Christmas and Easter.

What was I missing?

Thankfully, I wasn't the only person to ask these questions. In the last fifteen years, dozens of fascinating books have been written about God, the Bible and food. In addition to reading other books, I read Dr. Rex Russell's groundbreaking book, *What the Bible Says about Healthy Living*, which answered a lot of my questions. Of course God cares about what we eat! He intelligently designed our bodies, our digestive systems, our immune systems. And He intelligently designed our food: all types of plants and animals that perfectly match our bodies' nutritional needs.

I knew that other people struggled with food choices, so I began speaking about this topic at churches and women's events, which is how I met Amy, who sheepishly confessed that she had been eating and cooking "God's way" for most of her life and wanted to teach others how.

Within a few months, Amy and I started a monthly cooking club where we shared our wisdom and excitement about God's design for eating by actually cooking with a group of people. Each month we created recipes to cook and provided handouts of these recipes for each participant to take home. We were clearly onto something: why not take it a step further and publish our recipes? We did and this cookbook is the result.

Seeing the impact our recipes have had on

people's lives, we're convinced that God is at work, so we want to share our story with you. While we can't be in the kitchen with you personally, we can help you set up your kitchen and give you tasty recipes that are relatively simple to prepare.

We hope you enjoy our cookbook, and we hope you will share your success stories with us! Our prayer is that by submitting this area of your life to the One who created you, your life will be richly blessed and you will be a blessing to others.

Our Stories:
Amy Cataldo

Struggling to feed three kids—in a healthy way and on a budget—wasn't easy for Mom, who became a single parent when I was only six. So she joined a food co-op and our family's wonderful world of whole foods began: whole grain flour, pasta, nuts, dried fruit, nut butters and even weirder things, like nutritional yeast and textured vegetable protein.

Like Hope, I coveted my friends' Skippy and Smucker's sandwiches on white bread. I tried to trade my lunches for theirs, but no one was interested in brown bread or natural peanut butter. Eating my dried apricots, I quietly endured teasing and loud exclamations like, "Eeew! What is that?"

But Mom persisted, so I grew up eating home-cooked meals from scratch: if it came in a box, we probably didn't eat it. Thankfully, this upbringing conditioned my taste buds to prefer home-cooked, healthy meals, and I learned how to cook because of it. By junior high, my sister and I were regularly cooking dinner for the whole family.

When I started college in 1990, my busy schedule and tight budget forced me to change my eating habits. For the first time, I relied on cheap convenience foods, and I ate out more than I was used to, too: Pizza Hut pizza and sandwiches became staples. And when I expected to study until late, I often drank several large espressos before the night was over.

Even though I didn't eat horribly, I still missed healthy home-cooked meals. By graduation, I was looking forward to finding an apartment, having my own kitchen, and cooking from scratch again. For me, it tasted better, it was better for me, and I really loved doing it.

I landed a consulting job for a big firm, so I traveled constantly. Sadly, the return to my childhood eating patterns had to wait another four years. Meanwhile, I tried to make good food choices, but airline meals and hotel food left me few appealing alternatives.

Eventually I burned out. A slave to my job, I had no work-life balance. I was ready for a Change.

The need for Change—with a capital C—was more than just wanting a new job; I needed an entire lifestyle transformation. My work seemed meaningless and I felt physically sluggish from my travel-heavy lifestyle. I was also avoiding something that had been gnawing at me for several years: God. Was He real? Should He be part of my life?

Feeling paralyzed, I needed a kick-start. After reading the classic job-hunting guide *What Color Is Your Parachute?* and taking a formal aptitude test, it became clear that I was a natural teacher. I quit my job and entered an eight-week specialty program that helped business professionals become math and science teachers in the infamous Chicago public schools. In the fall of 1998, I started taking public transportation to work (an hour each way, often sitting on the bus with my high school students) and earning half of what I used to. It wasn't glamorous, but it was exactly what I needed.

Thankfully, my new lifestyle allowed me time to ponder my faith.

After my parents divorced when I was six, my mom found great comfort from God, so our home revolved around our Pentecostal church: we attended services Sunday morning, Sunday night and Wednesday night and youth group on Thursday night.

During this time I absorbed plenty of information about God, Jesus and the Bible. But this head knowledge sharply contradicted my actual experience: most churchgoers seemed hypocritical and legalistic. And after my dad died when I was fourteen, the church, as a whole, didn't love our family the way we needed to be loved. (In spite of the divorce, my dad was still a big part of our lives.)

The contradictions I saw at church and the pressure to attend so often, stifled any desire that I had to seek God or attend services on my own. I went to college and conveniently avoided church and anything related to it, including God.

As part of my life's overhaul in 1998, I realized that I had kept God on the shelf for long enough. I was sitting on the spiritual fence and it was time to make a decision about my faith, one way or another. I wanted to investigate the Bible in order to make up my own mind about God, so I joined a women's Bible study at Park Community Church in Chicago.

During that time I tangibly experienced God romancing me in a way that I can't explain. I soon claimed my own faith in Jesus (as opposed to something I merely inherited from my family or church). For me, it wasn't a huge stretch to admit that I fell short in many areas of my life and that I needed God to heal my wounded soul, or to believe that by turning to Him in faith He would heal me. But that was just the beginning: since then, I've been learning more and more about the God I have committed to and what this commitment means in my daily life.

Even now my struggles with the church haven't completely evaporated. But my faith in Christ has grown strong and I've felt a greater calling to care for my body as a gift from the One who created me. How do I do this? One way is by trying to understand God's design for eating. For example, I realized that even an occasional cup of coffee caused me to have severe withdrawal headaches when I wasn't drinking caffeine. I knew this probably wasn't God's design or desire for me, so I slowly weaned myself off of it.

A few years earlier I had started reading about healthy eating, and I began to understand all the scientific reasons why I ate the way I did. In 1997 I read *Spontaneous Healing* by Dr.

Andrew Weil, which explains that certain foods are actually toxic, while others are healthy and life-giving. Clearly, there was some intelligent design behind the foods that Mom fed us.

In January 2002 I read *What the Bible Says about Healthy Living* by Dr. Rex Russell. Now it made sense: not only does God care about me, but He also cares about what I eat and He designed food specifically for the human body. And after hearing Hope speak at our church, I knew that I wanted to partner with her to share this information with others. The rest—which you read in Hope's story—is history!

Another Great Resource from Hope Egan

Join best-selling author Hope Egan on her personal journey through what the Bible says about eating meat. Hope helps you see how science and Scripture brilliantly intertwine. Promoting neither legalism nor vegetarianism, *Holy Cow!* gently challenges you to take a fresh look at how you live out your faith!

PLUS: Man Alive! There's More!

Written by First Fruits of Zion educational director and Bible teacher D. Thomas Lancaster, Man Alive! delves further into some of the most challenging Scripture passages mentioned in the main part of this book. Fasten your seat belts and get out your Bibles; this may be the richest Scripture study you have ever experienced.

BOOK FEATURES!

- What the Bible says about eating meat
- Does science support the biblical food laws?
- Reconciling Old Testament meat passages with the New Testament
- Includes questions for group discussion or individual reflection

AUDIO CD

You'll feel like you're in the author's living room when you hear writer Hope Egan read *Holy Cow!* Egan is joined by master storyteller and First Fruits of Zion educational director D. Thomas Lancaster, who provides deep theological insights as Egan shares her personal journey through what the Bible says about eating meat.

Publisher: First Fruits of Zion
Pages: 161
Book: $14   CD: $25 (4-CD Set)
Bulk discounts available for purchases of 5 or more.
To order visit www.holycownews.com
or call First Fruits of Zion toll-free at 800-775-4807.

LaVergne, TN USA
18 November 2010

205320LV00006B/2/P